Encyclopedia of Mythical Creatures

Yokai & Japanese Mythology

An Illustrated Bestiary of Legendary Beasts, Oni, Monsters & Spirits from Ancient Worlds.

Created by:
Ziggy Quinete

Copyright© 2025 by Gargoyle Collective

All rights reserved. No part of this publication may be reproduced, stored or transmitted in any form or by any means, electronic, mechanical, photocopying, recording, scanning, or otherwise without written permission from the publisher. It is illegal to copy this book, post it to a website, or distribute it by any means without permission.

All brand names and product names used in this book and on its cover are trade names, service marks, trademarks and registered trademarks of their respective owners. The publishers and the book are not associated with any product or vendor mentioned in this book. None of the companies or countries referenced with the book have endorsed the book.

"Encyclopedia Mythical Creatures" is a work of fiction based on mythological creatures from around the world. The contents of this book, including but not limited to the descriptions, illustrations, and symbolism of myths, are intended for entertainment and educational purposes only. The authors and publishers make no claim to the accuracy or completeness of the information provided and are not responsible for any errors or omissions. This book should not be used as a reference for medical or psychological use, and no part of this book should be interpreted as medical advice. The interpretation and use of the book's contents are at the reader's own risk.

First Printing Edition, 2025
ISBN - 978-65-988087-8-5

Published by Gargoyle Collective
Author: Ziggy Quinete
Illustrations: Satoshi Watanabe

Nights through dreams tell the myths forgotten by the day.

— *C.G. Jung*

table of contents

Celestial & Divine Beings

Amabie.. 8
Amanozako.. 10
Ame-onna.. 12
Amikiri.. 14
Benzaiten's Serpent Aspect... 16
Bishamon's Tiger Guardian... 18
Byakko.. 20
Fujin.. 22
Hachiman's Doves... 24
Hakutaku... 26
Konohanasakuya.. 28
Raijin's Drumming Beast.. 30
Ryujin... 32
Suzaku.. 34
Tenjin's Thunder Bull.. 36
Tentei's Sky Hounds.. 38
Yatagarasu.. 40

Nature Spirits & Elemental Forces

Abura-sumashi.. 42
Akaname... 44
Azukiarai.. 46
Enenra.. 48
Furutsubaki-no-rei... 50
Hiderigami... 52
Hitodama.. 54
Jikininki.. 56
Kappa.. 58
Kawa-uso.. 60
Kodama... 62
Mokumokuren... 64
Namazu... 66
Nurarihyon.. 68
Raiju.. 70
Suiko... 72
Tsuchigumo... 74

Shapeshifters, Tricksters & Illusions

Bake-neko	76
Futa-kuchi-onna	78
Hannya	80
Hone-onna	82
Ittan-momen	84
Jorogumo	86
Kamaitachi	88
Kasa-obake	90
Kitsune	92
Mujina	94
Nure-onna	96
Obake-inu	98
Rokurokubi	100
Tanuki	102
Tesso	104
Yuki-onna	106
Yosuzume	108

Vengeful Spirits & Yokai of Death

Ao-andon	110
Funayurei	112
Gashadokuro	114
Ikiryo	116
Iso-onna	118
Jibakurei	120
Kuchisake-onna	122
Nopperabo	124
Oiwa	126
Onryo	128
Oni	130
Otoroshi	132
Shirime	134
Shinigami	136
Ubume	138
Yamauba	140

Animals, Guardians & Hybrid Beasts

Bake-kujira	142
Baku	144
Basan	146
Chimimoryo	148
Gyuki	150

Animals, Guardians & Hybrid Beasts (cont.)

Hebi-onna.. 152
Inugami... 154
Jatai.. 156
Kirin... 158
Nue.. 160
Ōmukade.. 162
Onikuma.. 164
Shachihoko... 166
Shikigami.. 168
Shojo... 170
Tengu.. 172
Umibozu.. 174
Ushioni... 176

the importance of myth

I have always believed myths are the world's oldest mirrors—of our soul. This book is an illustrated journey through one of our oldest myths and imagined creatures. They have inhabited the human history for millennia, and, in many ways, have shaped our own reality. They are a reflections of our collective fears, desires and subconscious.

Collecting these tales meant packing a suitcase with notebooks and curiosity, then following folklore trails from Andean peaks to Japanese coastlines. Every conversation—whether with a museum archivists, psychologists, and experts reminded me that myth is never just old: it is evergreen, bending and blooming with each retelling. I shaped each entry to show not only where a creature comes from but why it still matters in a world of satellites and smartphones.

Yet these stories would feel half-alive without images, and that's where the astonishing brush of Satoshi Watanabe enters. Satoshi's style captures fur, fang, and feather with equal tenderness; every spread feels like a portal you might accidentally step through if you lean too close. He created each creature expressly for this volume, and I'm still surprised each time I turn a finished page and feel the same childhood thrill of seeing a legend flicker into color.

My hope is that you will read with both skepticism and surrender—question the facts, yes, but let the wonder seep in all the same. Myths endure because they answer needs logic can't always satisfy: the longing for mystery, the comfort of metaphor, the thrill of recognizing ourselves in a dragon's eye or a mermaid's song. If the chapters ahead nudge you to keep a lookout for hoofprints where none should be or to listen closer when the wind changes, then these pages have done their job.

So travel lightly, reader, and step carefully: every myth you meet here has sharp teeth or gentle wisdom—sometimes both. And remember, the next story worth telling might be your own.

- Ziggy Quinete

amabie

celestial and divine beings
prophetic sea spirit

During the Edo Period, when the tides off Higo Province gleamed strangely bright, a single light broke the horizon — soft, green, and alive. It was not a ship's lantern nor a reflection of stars, but the living shimmer of a being rising from the sea. The fishermen who saw her could not name what they beheld: a creature with long hair like kelp in moonlight, scales that glowed like lacquered jade, and a face that seemed both gentle and unearthly. The world would later call her Amabie, the radiant one who speaks from the waves.

Eyewitnesses said her body resembled a young woman's but ended in a finned tail, each scale refracting pale light like wet glass. From her sides grew three translucent fins, symbols that would later be interpreted as the trinity of blessing, protection, and prophecy. She was neither monstrous nor divine but carried the beauty of something untamed, born of both sea and spirit. When she spoke, her voice was said to ripple across the water like the ringing of a shell.

Her words carried warning and mercy in equal measure. "A plague will come," she said, "but those who look upon my image shall remain unharmed." Then, before fear could take root, she sank beneath the darkening waves, leaving behind only her reflection trembling upon the surface. The official who heard her command obeyed faithfully, commissioning artists to capture her likeness in woodblock prints. Thus began the legend of the sea prophet who healed through art rather than medicine.

Across Japan, her face spread faster than rumor. Prints of Amabie appeared in marketplaces, on household doors, and even inside temples, carried by those who believed her gaze alone could ward off illness. Her scales became symbols of resilience, her fins of harmony between human and nature. Each copy of her portrait — crude or masterful — was an act of faith disguised as art, a reminder that creation itself can be a form of protection. Through ink and image, the people made a pact with the unseen.

As the years rolled forward and the age of wood gave way to the age of light, Amabie slipped quietly into myth. Yet when modern Japan faced new invisible threats, she rose once more, carried not by waves but by screens. Her visage flooded social media feeds instead of scrolls, a bright, beaked charm reborn in digital ink. From doctors' offices to street murals, her message reemerged: that to create and share beauty in dark times is to heal the soul of a nation.

Some scholars have speculated that Amabie might be kin to ancient sea deities — a fragment of the Dragon King's court or a forgotten water kami who once safeguarded fishermen. Others believe she embodies the sea's dual nature: the power to give life and to take it away. The triple fins, in this view, represent the balance between past, present, and future — her gift being foresight, her warning, compassion. Whatever her origin, her legend endures because it speaks to the human need for light when reason falters.

In artistic tradition, Amabie's features have been drawn a thousand ways: with bird-like feathers, with fish scales, with hair that spills across her shoulders like water itself. Every version carries her same serene gaze — calm, distant, unafraid. To draw her is to enter into the same ritual of protection begun in the Edo period, to conjure hope through color and line. She is not simply a mythic creature, but a living metaphor for the way imagination defies despair.

amanozako

celestial and divine beings
tempest of heaven's rage

Long before mortals learned to name the wind, an ancient fury took shape among the clouds. From the anger of the god Susanoo, who raged against the heavens and their order, was born a being that could not be contained — Amanozako, the storm's daughter and the embodiment of divine rebellion. Her birth was not gentle; she emerged screaming into the sky, her voice so shrill that mountains trembled and birds fell from their flight.

Legends tell that she inherited every violent emotion her father had cast away. Her teeth were long enough to tear iron, her hair wild as windblown seaweed, and her eyes burned gold with the ferocity of thunder. She carried in her heart the tempests of heaven and in her lungs the howling of ten thousand storms. Wherever she roamed, crops bowed, rivers surged backward, and men hid their faces lest her fury catch their gaze.

Yet Amanozako was not merely destruction. She was intellect sharpened by rage, a cunning spirit who mocked both gods and men. When celestial beings tried to restrain her, she laughed and vanished into the mountain passes, claiming the wilderness as her kingdom. Her laughter became the wind's voice, echoing through valleys after storms — a chilling reminder that no divine law could bind what was born from divine wrath itself.

In later ages, travelers feared the lands where her presence lingered. Shepherds in the provinces of Izumo and Ise spoke of a shadow that moved against the wind, with hair so long it brushed treetops and a face shifting between beauty and beast. If a person angered her, Amanozako would twist their heart, making them suspicious and stubborn. It was said she delighted in sowing quarrels among families, feeding on human spite the way storms feed on heat.

From her line came other troublesome spirits — the arrogant Amanojaku among them, those mischievous tricksters who defied morality and turned kindness into chaos. Through them, her legacy endured, infecting the world with a spark of divine disobedience. In this way, Amanozako stands not only as a figure of fear but also as the primordial source of all yokai born from defiance — those who refuse submission to heaven or man.

Some scholars saw in her story an echo of feminine power long vilified — a warning against women who speak too loudly, think too freely, or resist too fiercely. To them, Amanozako was the shadow of rebellion itself, the price of creation's imbalance. But to others, she became a symbol of unbroken will: the storm that would rather howl than bow, the voice that refuses silence.

Artists often paint her with wild hair and gleaming eyes that hold both madness and melancholy. Beneath the ferocity, they sense loneliness — the isolation of a creature too vast to belong to any realm. Her fury, they say, was never random but born from pain, from being misunderstood by the heavens that created her. In her storms lies the sorrow of exile, in her shriek the cry of something that once wished to be loved.

Old villagers still whisper her name into the gale. They know she cannot be appeased — only respected. Amanozako is the sky's mirror of human rage, the tempest that reminds even gods that creation is not born from serenity, but from the wild, ungovernable breath of chaos.

ame-onna

celestial and divine beings
weeping lady of the rain

There are nights in Japan when the rain falls with strange persistence — not as a storm, but as a mourning. In the narrow alleys of old towns, people once said that when the clouds refuse to clear, it is because a woman is weeping among them. That woman is Ame-onna, the rain spirit who wanders between heaven and earth, bringing both life and melancholy with every droplet she sheds.

Stories claim she appears during the heaviest rainfall, emerging suddenly from misty streets or forest paths. Her hair clings wet to her face, her kimono plastered to her thin body, and her eyes shine like dark pools. In one tale, she carries a small child in her arms — a ghostly infant that vanishes when lightning strikes. In another, she walks alone, forever seeking the child she once lost to the flood. Wherever she passes, the sky grows heavy, as if mirroring her sorrow.

Older traditions root her origin in the belief that excessive grief can call the rain. Some say Ame-onna was once a mortal woman who prayed endlessly for her vanished child until her tears joined the storm clouds above. Heaven, moved or burdened by her devotion, transformed her into a yokai condemned to cry for eternity. Her tears became rain itself, and her voice — the soft drumming of drops against rooftops — the sound of her endless lament.

In other regions, she is less tragic and more mischievous: a wanderer who brings rain to weddings, festivals, and journeys, ruining human joy out of spite or loneliness. Parents once warned their children not to mock the weather, for the rain could be listening — and if Ame-onna heard laughter beneath her clouds, she would pour until laughter turned to frustration. Her rain was a reminder that joy should never forget sorrow.

Artists throughout the Edo period found fascination in her duality. Some painted her as a ghostly mother, her figure half-transparent amid gentle drizzle; others showed her crouched by the roadside, scooping rainwater into her palms to drink her own tears. In every depiction, she remains both beautiful and mournful — a spirit who gives water to the world even as she drowns in her own memory.

To the poets, Ame-onna became a symbol of transient emotion — the soul's rain that nourishes and destroys alike. Her presence blurs the line between weather and feeling, turning each downpour into an act of remembrance. Haiku masters compared her tears to cherry blossoms falling too soon, a quiet sorrow that touches everyone yet belongs to no one.

There are those who still believe she visits the living. Travelers caught alone on mountain paths whisper thanks to the rain, fearing to anger her. In lonely cities, where neon light reflects in puddles, people speak of a woman's shadow lingering in the glass — drenched, weeping, and gone before the next blink. Perhaps Ame-onna no longer needs temples or prayers; perhaps she lives in the quiet hearts that still understand what it means to grieve for beauty lost.

Some rains cleanse, others remember. And when the night sky weeps without thunder or wind, only a soft, endless fall, it is said that the Ame-onna walks again — neither curse nor blessing, but the unending ache of love that refused to fade, falling gently through the centuries.

amikiri

celestial and divine beings

net-snipping spirit

Along Japan's mist-draped shores, where fishermen mend their nets by lantern light, stories whisper of a creature that creeps silently through the fog, cutting what men have woven. The people call it Amikiri — the Net-Cutter — a restless yokai whose delight lies in undoing the labors of others. Neither fish nor fowl, neither insect nor demon, it glides between worlds as easily as it severs their boundaries.

Witnesses describe a long, spindly body covered in shell plates that gleam like damp coral. Its head is crowned with a narrow beak sharp enough to slice silk, and its forelimbs end in claws that move with mechanical precision. By moonlight, the Amikiri appears almost graceful, drifting just above the surface of the sea, yet every motion carries quiet menace. When fishermen awake to find their nets shredded or their screens torn, they know the creature has passed in the night.

The earliest recorded mention appears in the Edo-period Gazu Hyakki Yagyō by Toriyama Sekien, who painted the Amikiri with playful ambiguity — perhaps a warning to those who trust too deeply in man-made order. Some villagers saw it as a trickster spirit punishing greed, others as a phantom of the sea jealous of human harvests. Whatever its motive, the damage it caused was never maliciously cruel; it simply cut for the sake of cutting, a force of disruption reminding mortals that nothing woven stays whole forever.

Sailors told of hearing faint snipping sounds in the dark, like scissors through wet paper, before storms rolled in. They said the Amikiri's presence foretold bad weather, its restless claws stirring the wind. Fishermen who chased it reported seeing only whirlpools where its body had been, as if the sea itself had folded shut behind it. Women working at looms feared it too, for it was said to slip inland on humid nights, slicing thread and silk as if mocking human imitation of the ocean's weave.

Not all accounts are fearful. Some coastal households left small offerings by their doors — pieces of rope tied loosely, inviting the spirit to satisfy its urge harmlessly. When the rope vanished or was found neatly severed, the family believed the Amikiri had accepted the gift, sparing their nets. This custom lingered in quiet fishing villages, a peculiar ritual of respect toward a creature no one truly hated, only dreaded with a resigned affection.

Folklorists have long debated whether the Amikiri is related to crustaceans like shrimp and crabs or to avian deities of cutting wind. Its hybrid form reflects the Japanese tendency to blend sea and sky, work and play, divine and absurd. Some scholars link its legend to the frustrations of fishermen, whose livelihoods depended on fragile tools constantly undone by tide and time. The Amikiri, then, becomes the embodiment of futility itself — a spirit that laughs at permanence.

Painters of the Meiji era reimagined it with almost comic charm: a long-nosed shrimp wielding scissors like a craftsman, its grin both wicked and whimsical. Yet beneath the humor lies quiet philosophy. Every snip it takes through rope or silk is a reminder that all nets — whether of twine, love, or fate — eventually fray. The Amikiri teaches humility through sabotage, offering chaos as a kind of wisdom.

benzaiten's serpent aspect

celestial and divine beings
goddess of flowing wisdom

On certain islands where shrine and sea touch, locals speak of a white serpent gliding silently through the water beneath the moon. The creature is said to be no mere snake but the living incarnation of Benzaiten, the goddess of music, eloquence, and the boundless flow of all things. Though worshiped in radiant temples, her serpent form belongs to the water's secret depth — a reminder that divinity can shimmer with both grace and terror.

In this aspect, Benzaiten embodies the union of beauty and primordial force. The serpent that coils around her is not a companion but her very essence — the divine made serpentine, the current of inspiration given flesh. In early syncretic Buddhism, she was likened to the Indian goddess Sarasvatī, whose sacred river carried wisdom; in Japan, that river became a serpent's body, winding through the mountains and lakes that fed human imagination. Her breath, they say, moves the strings of the biwa; her scales reflect the rhythm of rain.

Legends trace her serpent manifestation to the island of Enoshima, where Benzaiten descended to calm a monstrous dragon that plagued the land. When the beast fell in love with her, she did not reject its devotion but transformed it — merging divine compassion with serpentine power. From that day, the dragon's hunger became reverence, and Benzaiten's spirit took on the shape of the creature she had redeemed. The serpent, once feared as destroyer, was reborn as guardian of enlightenment and art.

Travelers visiting her island shrine often report dreams of snakes coiling gently around their arms, whispering songs without words. Fishermen believe the white eel-like shapes that twist through moonlit waves are her messengers, guardians of speech and song who glide unseen beneath boats. Some devotees wear snake-shaped talismans engraved with her name, trusting that her watery wisdom will protect them from drought, madness, and the silence of forgotten prayers.

Priests of Kamakura once described her dual nature in paradox: she brings both harmony and jealousy, both blessings and storms. To those who create without humility, she can send ruin — splitting strings, shattering voices, or calling up floods that drown their vanity. Yet for those who honor her flow, inspiration never ceases. The serpent in her body symbolizes this endless current, a force that destroys stagnation and renews vitality.

In temple art of the Edo period, she appears draped in white robes edged with serpent motifs, her hair streaked with silver like the foam of breaking waves. Sometimes the serpent curls from her shoulder and encircles her face like a halo, its eyes calm, its tongue a flicker of divine fire. These images capture the paradox at her heart: a goddess who is both muse and monster, serenity entwined with wildness.

Even now, in the shrines of Lake Biwa and Enoshima, white snakes are fed with milk and sake as her emissaries. Pilgrims bow to their sinuous forms, whispering wishes for creativity, eloquence, and safe passage across life's unpredictable tides. The serpents glide away in silence, their gleam a living echo of her unseen gaze.

bishamon's tiger guardian

celestial and divine beings
golden sentinel of wrath

When temple bells toll beneath the winter moon, monks whisper that somewhere beyond the veil of incense, a tiger walks beside the god of war. This creature — fierce, golden, and utterly silent — is Bishamon's Tiger Guardian, the living embodiment of divine vigilance. Born from the same flame that forged swords and prayers alike, it serves as both protector and punisher, stalking unseen through the boundaries of the sacred.

In Japanese esoteric Buddhism, Bishamonten, the god of warriors and northern protection, is never truly alone. His tiger is his will given flesh — an emanation of disciplined fury. Where Bishamon guards the four directions with jeweled pagoda and spear, the tiger enforces his justice with fang and roar. It is said to stride across storm clouds in the form of living lightning, its steps echoing like distant drums of war. Its breath carries the scent of temple smoke and blood mingled with iron, the perfume of devotion and conflict intertwined.

According to ancient scrolls of Shingon and Tendai lore, this celestial beast first appeared during an age of imbalance, when demons and arrogant kings defied the law of karma. Bishamon's compassion could not reach them, so his wrath took the form of the tiger — a manifestation that struck fear into beings blind to virtue. It prowled across battlefields and haunted the dreams of tyrants, its gaze a mirror that showed every hidden cruelty. Those who repented claimed to hear a low purr beneath their prayers, as though the tiger had accepted their surrender.

At temples dedicated to Bishamonten, statues of tigers guard the stairways and gates, their mouths frozen between snarl and chant. Devotees say these carvings are more than stone — that the god's true tiger moves through them at night, animating their eyes with faint amber fire. Offerings of sake and polished mirrors are left at their feet to honor the creature's dual nature: feral yet divine, untamed yet perfectly obedient to celestial law.

Some mountain monks claim to have glimpsed the guardian in meditation, appearing as a luminous silhouette coiled around the god's throne. Its stripes flicker like sutra lines, each marking a vow made by those who fought with courage and fell with dignity. To them, the tiger is not merely a beast but a scripture alive — a living page in the sacred chronicle of righteous struggle. When the tiger's roar echoes in a warrior's heart, fear dissolves into clarity, for its sound is said to purify hesitation and awaken resolve.

But the Tiger Guardian is not kind by nature. It tests faith through challenge, tearing down arrogance as easily as it rends demons. Those who invoke Bishamon's protection falsely — without sincerity or humility — find their paths beset by misfortune, as if mauled by unseen claws. Yet for the worthy, it appears in moments of greatest peril: in the arrow's pause before death, in the calm between strike and counterstrike. Its golden eyes are the last thing many soldiers of legend claimed to see before victory — or transcendence.

Art from the Kamakura period often depicted the guardian entwined with clouds and flame, its tail forming a circle that symbolized the eternal balance of destruction and creation. In these paintings, Bishamon's tiger is less an animal than an idea — the very embodiment of shinnen, the focused spirit that conquers chaos.

byakko

celestial and divine beings
celestial white tiger

In the vast map of the heavens, where gods and beasts form constellations to guard the balance of creation, one prowls with unmatched majesty. This is Byakko, the White Tiger of the West — a spirit of autumn wind, metal, and righteous strength. To the ancient onmyōji, he was not merely a star's guardian but the very embodiment of divine order, his breath the gust that cleansed corruption from the world.

Where Seiryu, the Azure Dragon, coils through the East as spring's renewal, Byakko reigns over the twilight of the year. His domain is the season of falling leaves, of sharpened blades, and of clarity after harvest. The samurai revered him as the spirit of purity through struggle — destruction made sacred through purpose. His roar is said to scatter demons, his stride to flatten mountains, yet his heart remains calm as snow resting upon a blade's edge.

In the oldest texts of Chinese cosmology — later adopted by Japanese esoteric schools — Byakko stands as one of the Shijin, the Four Symbols born from cosmic breath. He guards the western skies and rules over the element of metal, which gleams and cuts yet never corrupts. To the Japanese, he became both divine emblem and living presence. Temples facing westward sometimes placed a tiger statue at their gates, believing that even a sculpture of his likeness could repel spirits of decay.

Monks wrote that when the world falls into chaos, Byakko descends from the Milky Way in the form of a white wind. Those who have seen him describe not an animal, but a force — a shimmer of fur and silver light, a presence that makes the air hum. It is said that when he walks, every sound sharpens: leaves crackle like metal, waves hiss like drawn swords, and hearts beat in rhythm with the pulse of truth itself.

Yet Byakko's nature is not only martial. To poets, he represents integrity, the virtue of standing firm in fading light. Just as the west holds the dying sun, he embodies endings that are dignified rather than tragic — the beauty of last moments, the calm strength of acceptance. Warriors once prayed to him before entering battle, asking not for victory but for clarity of mind, to meet fate without fear or regret.

Some tales claim he was born from the breath of the god of metal himself, while others describe him as the tiger-form of Amaterasu's shadow — the moon's reflection of the sun's courage. In either version, he is balance incarnate: power guided by restraint, ferocity bound by celestial law. Where his roar travels, the restless find peace, and where his paw falls, evil cannot root.

Shrines in Kyushu and Nara still preserve his symbols: white tigers painted on paper charms, silver calligraphy marking western walls. Pilgrims leave offerings of polished steel mirrors, their reflections catching the light as a silent invocation to his eternal watch. To glimpse a tiger-shaped cloud at dusk is considered a sign of protection, a reminder that Byakko still walks the edge between heaven and the mortal world.

In the end, Byakko is not a creature of wrath but of guardianship. His roar calls courage from the timid and silence from the proud. He is the final breath before the season turns, the gleaming twilight between life and death. And when the wind from the west grows cold and pure, those who listen closely may hear him move — a whisper of fur and thunder, prowling forever along the horizon of eternity.

fujin

celestial and divine beings
wild god of the wind

Long before human temples rose from the earth, the sky was ruled by two brothers — Fujin, master of wind, and Raijin, lord of thunder. Together they carved chaos into rhythm, teaching the heavens to breathe. Of the two, Fujin was the older and the freer, the laughter in the storm and the sigh between waves. His power was not the violence of destruction but the restless movement that makes the world alive.

Legends say he was born at the dawn of creation when Izanagi opened the gate of the underworld and the winds escaped from his sleeve. From that torrent came Fujin, roaring into the newborn world, his green skin streaked with stormlight and his laughter shaking the mountains. Carrying his great bag of winds, he released gales across the islands, shaping coastlines, scattering seeds, and giving breath to every creature that would one day walk the earth.

His image appears carved on ancient temple doors: a muscular, demon-faced figure leaping through the sky, his bulging sack slung over one shoulder. In one hand he opens the mouth of the bag to unleash gusts; in the other he steadies it, controlling chaos with deft precision. To peasants, he was both a blessing and a curse — the one who cleared clouds for harvest, yet also the one who could strip fields bare with a careless breath.

Tales from the Heian and Kamakura eras describe him as mischievous, even joyful, chasing Raijin across the heavens in games that sometimes erupted into typhoons. Their laughter was thunder; their footfalls, rolling wind. Yet when tempests struck too fiercely, monks climbed temple steps to pray, striking bells to calm his spirit. Fujin was not cruel, only indifferent to the boundaries of human peace.

Sailors feared him most. When gales rose suddenly at sea, they would hurl offerings of rice and sake into the foam, calling his name with both reverence and terror. The sea breeze that filled their sails was his gentler side — a whisper of favor. But when squalls tore the masts apart, they saw his grin in the clouds, teeth flashing like lightning, delighting in the raw freedom of the storm.

In mythic art, Fujin often appears alongside Raijin atop temple roofs, eternally chasing one another around the world's edge. The wind god's green body coils like a whirlwind, his bag swelling with invisible pressure. These statues are not merely decoration: they are guardians against stagnation, embodiments of nature's vitality. By letting the wind move freely, temples invite purification, for stagnation — of air, of spirit, of thought — is the true enemy of harmony.

Even today, Fujin is invoked in seasonal festivals when the wind shifts from warm to cold. Farmers in northern Japan still recite old songs asking him to "shake the sky gently." Artists, too, honor him — for he is the unseen muse behind all things that flow: music, fabric, words, and breath itself. To live in his favor is to live without stillness, to embrace change as sacred rhythm.

At sunset, when the wind sweeps through bamboo groves and the sky burns copper, listeners sometimes hear a deep chuckle among the rustling leaves. The old storytellers say that Fujin is passing by — not to punish or to bless, but simply to remind the world that movement is life. His laughter, they say, is the echo of creation still spinning, the storm's heart beating within the calm.

hachiman's doves

celestial and divine beings
messengers of divine peace

When the clamor of battle faded and banners drooped in the still air, there were said to appear two doves above the field — gliding silently through the smoke. The sight of them meant that Hachiman, the god of archery and war's virtue, had withdrawn his wrath and granted mercy. These were no common birds but his messengers, spirits of reconciliation born from the heart of conflict itself.

In the chronicles of the Heian and Kamakura eras, when warlords raised shrines to the god of warriors, white doves began nesting beneath their roofs. No matter how fierce the battles that raged outside, these birds remained untouched, their wings unruffled by the wind of arrows. The priests said they carried the prayers of the living to the god himself, their flight a thread binding heaven and battlefield. To see them circle above a temple after prayer was a sign that Hachiman had heard.

The Nihon Shoki speaks of Hachiman descending from the heavens as a radiant being flanked by doves, his heralds announcing his arrival. From that time forward, every temple built in his honor bore carvings of the birds — not as ornaments, but as divine intermediaries. They became the symbol of both protection and restraint, reminding those who worshiped him that victory meant nothing without compassion to follow it.

Over time, the doves came to embody the gentler side of martial virtue. Warriors prayed not only for triumph but for the grace to wield power justly, to know when to fight and when to yield. A general who ignored the flight of Hachiman's Doves risked divine displeasure, for their wings were said to stir the winds that carried arrows astray. Thus, even amid war, their presence whispered of peace waiting to return.

In art, they are often painted in pairs — one alighting, one ascending — reflecting the eternal cycle of war and restoration. Their feathers gleam faintly gold, symbolizing purity tempered by wisdom. On shrine banners, they hover above the god's mon, the circular crest that represents both the full moon and the target of the archer's perfect aim. It is said that when Hachiman draws his bow, the doves guide the arrow — not toward death, but toward destiny fulfilled.

There are stories from rural Japan of flocks of doves appearing over temples during times of unrest. Priests interpreted them as the god's silent call for restraint, urging humans to remember that peace is not weakness but mastery. Some accounts tell of wounded soldiers who, upon hearing the soft flutter of wings, laid down their weapons and found the strength to live differently. In this way, the birds became more than divine symbols — they were redemption given form.

Even now, at Usa Shrine in Kyushu, where Hachiman's worship first took root, white doves still gather near the torii gates. Pilgrims offer them grains and murmur thanks, for their presence is considered proof that the god still watches over Japan's spirit. When the wind stirs through their wings, one can almost hear the sigh of the old battle god himself — weary of blood, yearning for balance.

Whenever doves cross the sky in silence after a storm, the faithful remember the lesson of their lord: that power without mercy is hollow, and that true victory is found not in conquest but in the stillness that follows — the quiet flutter of wings beneath a sun restored.

hakutaku

celestial and divine beings

white marsh sage

In a distant age when the line between god and mortal still shimmered faintly, a radiant beast appeared before a great emperor. It rose from a field of white reeds as dawn broke, its mane glistening like dew and nine golden eyes watching from its head and sides. This being called itself Hakutaku — the White Marsh Spirit — a creature of divine intelligence who knows every demon, every illness, and every cure that exists beneath heaven. Its coming was not an omen of disaster, but of enlightenment.

The story tells that the Emperor of China, struck by strange dreams, went out to purify himself beside the sea. There, the Hakutaku emerged from mist and bowed its head. For three nights and days, it spoke without pause, revealing the names and natures of twelve thousand demons and the herbs that could banish them. The emperor ordered scribes to write every word, and thus was born the Hakutaku-zu, a sacred compendium of medicine and spirit lore said to safeguard nations. In Japan, the tale took root deeply, transforming the creature into a symbol of healing and foresight.

When plagues swept through the countryside, villagers painted its likeness on paper charms and hung them upon their doors. The Hakutaku's many eyes, they believed, could see the invisible — the origins of disease, the whispers of corruption in air and soul alike. Its image was said to frighten demons of pestilence and guide lost spirits back toward the light. Even those who had never seen it swore that its presence could be felt in the calm that followed a fever's breaking, or the cool wind that entered a room after prayer.

Descriptions of the creature vary across centuries. Some depict it with the body of a white ox, its nine eyes arranged like constellations upon its flanks; others see it as a leonine sage cloaked in mist. In Buddhist interpretation, it is sometimes viewed as a manifestation of compassionate wisdom, akin to Kannon's infinite sight. To scholars, it became an allegory for moral vigilance — that true wisdom is not the power to destroy evil, but to understand it completely.

Artists of the Edo period painted the Hakutaku with quiet reverence. Unlike the roaring dragons or fiery demons of other scrolls, it stands serenely upon pale clouds, its expression one of infinite patience. Around it float delicate ink characters representing purity, truth, and health. Many homes kept such images as talismans; if disease struck, offerings of rice and incense were placed beneath its portrait in hopes that its all-seeing eyes would intercede.

In temples, priests whispered that the Hakutaku rarely appears to mortals. When it does, it chooses only those whose hearts mirror its own — rulers, healers, or monks burdened by compassion. To encounter it is both blessing and burden, for it imparts knowledge so vast it can drive a mortal mind to silence. Those who claimed to dream of its voice spoke of it as a wind through bamboo, neither gentle nor harsh, filled with unending names.

Even in the modern age, the White Marsh Spirit endures as a symbol of science and faith entwined. During epidemics, its image reappeared in newspapers and charms, echoing Amabie's role as protector. Yet while Amabie brings hope through vision, Hakutaku brings reason through understanding — the wisdom to face the unseen without fear. It reminds humankind that enlightenment is not a gift from the heavens, but a discipline born of empathy.

konohanasakuya

celestial and divine beings

blossom princess

In the first days of Japan's divine age, when gods walked the mountains as easily as men tread upon fields, there bloomed from the earth a maiden so radiant that the cherry blossoms turned toward her light. She was Konohanasakuya-hime, the Princess Who Blossoms Like the Trees of Flowers — daughter of the mountain god Ōyamatsumi and the mortal reflection of spring itself. Wherever her feet touched, petals unfolded. Wherever she gazed, frost melted into life.

Her story begins not in serenity but in testing. When the god Ninigi — grandson of the sun goddess Amaterasu — descended from the heavens to claim the land, he met Konohanasakuya beside a river shining with morning dew. Struck by her grace, he asked for her hand. Her father, delighted, offered also her elder sister Iwanaga-hime, the Rock Princess, who symbolized endurance. But Ninigi refused the unadorned stone and chose only the flower. From that choice bloomed beauty — and impermanence. The gods decreed that, because he had chosen the blossom over the rock, the lives of his descendants, humankind, would bloom brightly but fade swiftly.

Though her husband's decision bound mortals to mortality, Konohanasakuya bore her fate with quiet dignity. When Ninigi doubted her faithfulness — suspecting that her sudden pregnancy was fathered by another god — she answered with fire. Retreating into a small hut, she sealed herself inside and set it ablaze, declaring that if her child were divine, she and the infant would survive unscathed. The flames consumed everything but her, for her purity burned brighter than the inferno itself. From that trial she emerged with her newborn sons, their skin untouched, their hearts radiant with celestial blood.

Since that day, she has been venerated as both goddess of blossoms and guardian of sacred birth. Temples dedicated to her dot the slopes of Mount Fuji and the volcanic peaks of Kyushu, places where life and destruction coexist. Her flame became a metaphor for transformation — that beauty is strongest not when it endures, but when it passes and returns renewed. To farmers, her favor meant fertile soil after fire; to poets, she embodied the sadness and splendor of transience.

Depictions of Konohanasakuya-hime vary: in some, she stands crowned with blossoms that fall endlessly but never touch the ground; in others, she carries a newborn wrapped in silk and ash. Artists of the Heian era painted her with a subtle melancholy — not sorrow, but the wisdom of one who knows that even perfection must wither. Her smile in these scrolls is faint, like dawn breaking through fog.

Festivals in her honor mark the coming of spring. As the first cherry petals drift through the air, devotees visit her shrines to pray for safe childbirth, long life, and beauty unmarred by vanity. Offerings of blossoms, rice wine, and white silk are made in gratitude for her gentle watching. When petals fall into rivers and vanish downstream, it is said that she carries them back to Mount Fuji, where they are reborn as snow.

Philosophers have long seen in her myth the essence of mono no aware — the deep awareness of impermanence that defines Japanese aesthetics. Through her, life's fragility is not a curse but a gift, for only fleeting things can be fully cherished. Her mountain stands eternal, yet she teaches that even eternity must breathe, bloom, and fade.

raijin's drumming beast

celestial and divine beings

rhythm of divine thunder

When lightning splits the sky and rain begins to tremble on rooftops, the old monks say that it is not the god Raijin himself who strikes the first note, but his companion — the Drumming Beast, the living pulse of the storm. Born from the echo of the first thunder ever heard, this creature runs ahead of its master, stirring the heavens like a musician tuning the world before performance. Its sound is the breath of the tempest, its roar the heartbeat of divine chaos.

Legends describe it as neither god nor yokai, but a manifestation — the sound given body. Where Raijin represents command and order over thunder, the beast is pure energy unrestrained, dancing across the firmament to awaken the storm's spirit. Its form changes as swiftly as weather: sometimes a lion with drums upon its back, sometimes a massive oni wrapped in cloud, sometimes little more than wind shaped into fury. All forms share the same essence — rhythm incarnate.

In ancient scrolls of the Heian period, it is said that this beast first emerged when Raijin lost his patience with silence. To break the stillness that smothered the world, he tore a bolt of lightning in half, and from that fracture leapt the Drumming Beast. Since then, it has never stopped moving. It rolls thunder over mountains, beats waves against cliffs, and sends ripples through the rice fields before rain arrives. Farmers listened for its distant drumming as a promise of renewal — that the parched earth would soon awaken.

Temples devoted to Raijin often depict the beast as the first sound that bridges heaven and earth. Wooden carvings above shrine gates show it chasing Raijin through the clouds, both surrounded by swirling golden drums. In these sculptures, one can almost feel the rhythm captured in motion — Raijin as the conductor, the beast as the percussion of creation itself. Drummers at festivals sometimes invoke its spirit by striking taiko in spiraling rhythms, believing that their music can echo the cosmic tempo and summon its blessing.

The beast's power is not solely destructive. To those who understand its rhythm, it offers protection. Monks chant in thunder rhythm to ward off evil spirits, and blacksmiths claim their finest blades are forged in the seconds between its drumbeats, when sound itself still vibrates in the air. Even the lightning that splits trees is considered its signature, a brushstroke of divine percussion across the landscape.

Travelers tell of hearing the beast during sleepless nights — a soft, distant drumming just before a storm. Some say it walks invisible among the clouds, others that it beats the sky's edge to drive away demons that feed on silence. It is not anger that moves it, but purpose: to keep the world awake, alive, and responsive. The silence that follows its departure is not emptiness but renewal, as though the air itself has been cleansed by music.

In Edo-era prints, the Drumming Beast is portrayed with wild eyes and a grin of exhilaration, surrounded by curling ribbons of wind. Artists painted lightning as arcs of pure calligraphy, transforming thunder into art. Through these depictions, it became a symbol of creative fury — the energy that shatters stillness so that new life may rise. To invoke it is to invite change, to welcome the unpredictable power that both destroys and inspires.

ryūjin

celestial and divine beings
dragon god of the sea palace

Far beneath the mirror of the waves lies Ryūgū-jō, the Palace of the Dragon King, where coral pillars glow like fire beneath water and the floor is paved with shells that whisper the music of the tides. Here dwells Ryūjin, the dragon god of the sea — ancient, sovereign, and endlessly watchful. He commands every current, every storm, and every creature that glides through the abyss. His presence is both tranquil and terrifying, for the same hand that calms the waves can summon their wrath.

According to the Kojiki and Nihon Shoki, Ryūjin was born when the primordial waters first stirred under heaven's gaze. His form stretches beyond measure, serpentine yet graceful, a living river of scales that shimmer from green to gold. In his jaws he carries the tide jewels, sacred orbs that govern ebb and flow. With the Kanju he summons the rising tide; with the Manju he draws it back. Through these twin treasures, he binds the breathing of the world to the sea's eternal rhythm.

When Hoori, ancestor of emperors, lost his brother's fishhook, it was Ryūjin's daughter, the sea princess Toyotama-hime, who brought him to the palace of pearls. There the dragon king welcomed the mortal with feasts of shimmering fish and songs older than language. In gratitude, he granted Hoori one of the tide jewels — and with it, dominion over sea and storm. From this union of man and sea-deity sprang the imperial bloodline, linking the throne of Japan to the ocean's pulse.

Yet Ryūjin's benevolence is never guaranteed. To sailors who respect the sea, he grants smooth passage and full nets; to the arrogant, he sends whirlpools and thunder. His moods mirror the ocean itself — serene one moment, ruthless the next. The old priests taught that when a typhoon roars across the coast, it is the god turning in his sleep. Offerings of rice wine and abalone were cast into the surf to soothe him, lest his dreams break upon the shore.

Artists of the Heian and Edo periods often painted him as both god and beast — half-man, half-dragon, seated upon a throne of shell and coral, his long white beard mingling with the waves. In his hand rests the gleaming jewel, the nyoi-hōju, symbol of enlightenment and control over desire. Around him swim turtle courtiers, jellyfish attendants, and fish that shimmer like living gems. In these works, Ryūjin is less a tyrant than a monarch of balance, embodying the unity of beauty and danger that defines the sea.

Scholars have long seen him as the Japanese reflection of ancient ocean deities across Asia — cousin to the Chinese Longwang and echo of the Indian Varuna. Yet his character is uniquely Japanese: intimate, local, shaped by fishermen's prayers and volcanic coastlines. He is not distant divinity but the neighbor of every wave, listening to nets drawn through foam, breathing with each tide's return.

Those who visit seaside shrines dedicated to him — especially the Ryūjin shrines of Izu and Enoshima — still bring shells or pearls as offerings. On certain nights, priests claim to see his reflection flicker in the surf: a gleam of gold eyes beneath the water, a quick shiver of light before vanishing into dark.

At dawn, when the horizon blurs silver and the sea inhales the light of the sun, the old fishermen bow toward the east and whisper his name. They say the dragon never truly sleeps; he dreams of tides yet to come, of stars mirrored in water, of mortals who still remember the balance between reverence and greed.

suzaku

suzaku

celestial and divine beings

vermilion bird of the heavens

In the ancient skies, where constellations were gods and the winds themselves carried meaning, the southern quadrant blazed with living flame. From that fiery realm came Suzaku, the Vermilion Bird, guardian of the South and embodiment of the summer sun. She is the fire that gives life as easily as it consumes, the eternal spark of transformation woven through heaven's design.

Her feathers are said to shimmer with every hue of sunset — red fading to gold, gold softening into rose, rose vanishing into white. When she flies, heat follows her like a hymn, and the sky ripples with the color of renewal. In the ancient Chinese cosmology of the Shijin, later embraced by Japanese esoteric tradition, Suzaku represents the element of fire and the virtue of propriety: the order of beauty, the discipline within passion. To behold her, even in dream, was to witness harmony between destruction and rebirth.

Myths tell that Suzaku first revealed herself to the Emperor of Heaven during the world's first midsummer solstice. As the air shimmered with unbearable heat, a single feather descended — soft, incandescent, unburned — and from that feather rose the song of creation. Since that moment, the Vermilion Bird has been the voice of time's renewal, the phoenix that never dies because it is forever becoming. Her presence marks eras of peace and prosperity, when the world burns only to bloom again.

Priests of ancient Kyoto, following the ways of yin and yang, placed her shrine to the south, opposite Byakko's western temple, so that flame would balance metal, warmth would temper strength. In those days, the emperor's palaces were built with the "Suzaku Gate" facing south, a symbolic gesture inviting light, fortune, and divine guidance into the realm. Her wings became metaphors for enlightenment and justice — radiant, but always measured by grace.

Artists of the Heian and Edo periods rendered her as a firebird gliding through clouds of incense, her tail unfurling like silk banners in the wind. Unlike her Western cousin, the phoenix, Suzaku does not rise from ash — she is the perpetual flame that never dies, existing in continuity rather than resurrection. Scrolls portray her carrying small orbs of light within her talons, believed to be the souls of seasons themselves, kindled and released as time turns.

Though celestial in origin, Suzaku's warmth touches the human world. To farmers, her domain governs the ripening of grain; to poets, she is the muse of summer's radiance and exhaustion alike. Her song is said to summon not fire but awareness — the sudden realization that all living things burn in their own way, whether by love, duty, or the simple passage of days. Through that flame, she teaches that passion and impermanence are one and the same.

Some legends say she alights on Mount Kōya once every thousand years, bathing the mountain in red light that turns leaves to gold. Monks who meditate beneath the trees on such nights claim to hear wings in the wind, followed by an overwhelming peace, as though every thought had been set aflame and purified. For them, Suzaku is not a goddess to be worshipped but a truth to be endured — that enlightenment comes only through surrender to change.

tenjin's thunder bull

celestial and divine beings

storm-bringer

When thunder rolls over Kyoto's northern hills, old scholars bow their heads and whisper not in fear, but in reverence. They say the sound is not mere weather — it is the hooves of Tenjin's Thunder Bull, the divine mount of the god of scholarship and storms, galloping across the heavens. Born from divine injustice and elevated through genius, Tenjin's wrath took form in this celestial beast, which now carries the memory of both vengeance and enlightenment.

The story begins with Sugawara no Michizane, a brilliant poet and minister of the Heian court. Betrayed by rivals and exiled unjustly to Kyushu, his spirit, once gentle as ink and verse, transformed into the deity Tenjin upon his death. As the storms that followed his passing ravaged the capital, the people realized the winds bore not malice, but divine lament. Lightning cracked the skies as though the heavens themselves sought retribution. From those tempests came the Bull — a being of thunder, loyalty, and unbroken mind.

In the earliest scrolls, the Thunder Bull appears as a massive black ox whose horns glow like molten gold. It emerged beside Tenjin's shrine after the god's enshrinement, bellowing with thunder each time prayers of injustice were spoken. The creature's breath carried static; its hooves struck sparks that ignited the rain. Priests believed it was the living conduit of Tenjin's emotion — his rage against corruption, his sorrow for lost honor, and his unending devotion to truth.

Over time, the Bull became symbol of Tenjin's mercy as well as his power. Where once it stormed through the skies in fury, it now walks beside the god as his patient steed, guiding him through tempests with steadfast calm. In art, Tenjin is often depicted seated upon a reclining ox, his expression serene, his robe rippling in invisible wind. The beast's bowed head represents humility before wisdom, reminding mortals that true strength lies in submission to learning — even for gods.

During storms, families once left plum blossoms and inkstones on their altars, asking the Thunder Bull to shield their homes from lightning. Students, too, offered small clay figures of oxen before examinations, believing that the divine mount could carry their prayers to Tenjin's celestial court. To hear thunder on the eve of a test was seen not as bad omen, but as blessing — the Bull stirring in acknowledgment.

Poets of the Edo era described the Bull as the soul of perseverance, its muscles forged from the patience of scholars and its heart from divine outrage. In one poem, it is said that each bolt of lightning that cleaves the sky is the Bull's hoofprint, marking the heavens with lessons too vast for parchment. Painters captured this duality: eyes fierce yet compassionate, body bound by lightning yet unmoving, an image of wisdom held steady within chaos.

At Kitano Tenmangū, the great shrine dedicated to Tenjin in Kyoto, statues of reclining oxen line the paths. Pilgrims stroke their heads to absorb the god's intelligence, believing the Bull's calm will quiet their own restless minds. Children learn to whisper wishes into its ears before studying, trusting that every spark of understanding is a trace of lightning tamed by faith.

tentei's sky hounds

celestial and divine beings
thunder coursers of heavenly law

Long before mortals charted constellations, the sky was said to be patrolled by radiant beasts that answered only to Tentei, the Celestial Emperor who governs order above the clouds. These were the Sky Hounds, swift as thought, tireless as the wind. They roamed the borders of heaven, guarding the constellations from chaos and devouring wayward stars before they could fall and seed calamity below. When thunder rolled without rain, people said it was the sound of their pursuit — divine paws striking the vault of the firmament.

Their birth was written in lightning. When the first storm split the heavens, Tentei gathered the shards of light that scattered across the void and breathed into them the breath of command. From those fragments sprang the hounds — luminous, fanged, and bound to the pulse of thunder. Each beat of their hearts echoed with the rhythm of the celestial drums. Their duty was sacred and endless: to hunt disobedient spirits of the sky, those that fled the Emperor's law to tempt humankind with forbidden fire.

Ancient priests claimed that meteors were the sparks thrown from the hounds' claws as they bounded through the clouds. The streaks that followed them across the night were neither comets nor stars, but the paths of their divine chase. When one fell to earth, it was believed that a fragment of divine law had broken loose — a sign that heaven's order wavered and must be restored through ritual. Thus, temples lit sacred fires when meteors crossed the sky, calling the hounds back to their master's leash.

In paintings of the Nara and Heian courts, the Sky Hounds appear as elegant, almost leonine dogs, their bodies surrounded by spiral motifs symbolizing wind and motion. Their eyes are never angry, only resolute — guardians who destroy not for pleasure but for balance. To behold them in vision was considered a mark of divine favor, a reminder that duty need not be cruel when it is guided by justice.

Travelers in later centuries told quieter tales. In mountain passes shrouded by storm, herders sometimes heard distant barking that rose and fell with the thunder. They left offerings of sake and salt upon stones, whispering thanks for unseen protection. For while Tentei ruled the stars, his hounds ruled the weather; their breath drove away plague winds and their growl dispersed malignant ghosts that fed upon night mists.

Some monks saw in them a lesson for humanity — that loyalty, when bound to truth, becomes holiness. The hounds, though mighty enough to swallow constellations, remained servants to a single command: keep the heavens pure. Their restraint was their glory. In temple poetry, they are described as the silence between storms, guardians whose strength lies in obedience rather than rebellion.

Artists of the Edo period revived their imagery, painting them racing alongside thunder gods Raijin and Fūjin, bridging Shinto and Buddhist cosmologies. In these works the hounds are caught mid-stride, tongues of flame curling from their jaws, eyes reflecting the Milky Way itself. They became symbols of divine vigilance — reminders that even the wildest forces in nature answer to harmony when guided by rightful purpose.

When thunder murmurs on clear nights and no rain follows, elders still lift their eyes to the stars and smile. "Tentei's hounds are running," they say, "keeping heaven clean." In that sound of distant thunder, echoes the oldest promise between order and freedom: that even the storm must serve the light.

yatagarasu

celestial and divine beings
divine guidance

When the mists of myth first parted above the land of Yamato, a single dark shape descended from the sun. Its feathers gleamed like lacquer, its wings beat with quiet thunder, and its three legs struck the air in a rhythm older than speech. The people called it Yatagarasu — the "eight-span crow" — emissary of Amaterasu, sent to lead emperors and wanderers alike toward their rightful path.

Legends tell that when Emperor Jimmu, the first ruler of Japan, lost his way in the mountains of Kumano, this strange crow appeared before his army. It did not speak, yet every motion of its wings pointed toward the plains of Yamato, where his destiny awaited. For seven days it flew ahead of him, pausing upon branches and stones until the weary soldiers could follow. When they reached their promised land, the bird vanished into sunlight, leaving only the faint smell of rain and ash. Thus began its legacy as the divine navigator — a being whose appearance meant that heaven itself was paying attention.

In the oldest interpretations, Yatagarasu's three legs represent the trinity of heaven, earth, and humanity — or, in the imperial reading, the virtues of wisdom, benevolence, and valor. To onmyōji astrologers, it symbolized the sun's motion through dawn, noon, and dusk; to the priests of Kumano, it was a living embodiment of divine will moving through natural law. Each tradition saw in its third leg not deformity but perfection — balance achieved through asymmetry.

Descriptions of its form differ across eras. Some see it as a giant bird whose wings blot out the sun, each feather edged in fire; others imagine a smaller crow that perches unnoticed until it is needed. Both are true in spirit: Yatagarasu is less creature than presence. It arrives not to speak, but to correct the course of those who have strayed — kings, priests, travelers, and the lost alike. Where the crow flies, confusion ends.

In medieval Japan, samurai banners sometimes bore its sigil, a black three-legged bird within a red sun. To march beneath that image was to claim divine direction — to move not by chance, but by purpose sanctified. Yet those who invoked it without sincerity risked disaster, for the crow's favor cannot be demanded. It reveals truth only to those willing to change upon seeing it.

At the Kumano shrines of Wakayama, pilgrims still trace their journeys by the path of the crow. Amulets depicting its silhouette promise guidance and safety in travel, while priests speak of hearing the rustle of invisible wings during prayer. When a sudden shadow passes across the torii gate at sunrise, they say Yatagarasu has flown overhead, confirming that the gods remain attentive.

To poets, it is not only guide but revelation — the spark that bridges ignorance and enlightenment. Its black feathers mirror the night from which wisdom emerges; its flight follows the line of the horizon where heaven meets earth. Painters often depict it carrying a sphere of light in its beak, a symbol of understanding drawn from darkness.

And when dusk settles over the mountains and a single crow cries out against the dying light, villagers still pause and bow their heads. For in that cry they hear the echo of Yatagarasu's ancient mission — to remind the living that the way is never truly lost, only waiting for courage to follow the next wingbeat toward the sun.

abura-sumashi

nature spirits and elemental forces

oil thief

In the quiet hills of Kumamoto, when twilight pools beneath the cedars and the fog creeps down from the ridges, travelers speak of a small figure waiting by the roadside. He does not move at first — merely watches, round-headed, silent, and still as a stone. Then, when the wind shifts, he seems to breathe, and his strange, gravelly voice murmurs a greeting no one remembers clearly. This is Abura-sumashi, the spirit of the oil thief, doomed to haunt the path between village and forest for all eternity.

His name means "oil presser," but his story is one of theft and repentance. Long ago, lamp oil was sacred — drawn from precious rapeseed or fish, kept for shrines and temple lamps that burned before the gods. To steal such oil was not mere robbery but sacrilege, an act that darkened one's spirit as surely as night devours flame. The villagers tell that a man once crept into a shrine by lantern light to siphon the offering oil for his own use. When he died, his soul could find no rest, weighed down by what he had stolen from the divine. Thus he returned, transformed — his head turned to stone, his body wrapped in rough straw, condemned to wander forever in half-light.

Those who meet him on the old mountain road describe him as neither frightening nor kind. His face, gray and coarse as river rock, bears no emotion, yet his eyes gleam with something like regret. He moves slowly, as though burdened by invisible chains, and when he speaks, it is said that his voice echoes like wind through a clay jar. He asks no favors, seeks no revenge. He only watches the living pass — the travelers, the pilgrims, the children carrying lanterns up from the valley — as if reminding them to tread with reverence.

In some tales, he greets those who walk too boldly through his forest, warning them of the slippery paths ahead. In others, he appears beside fires that have burned too long, whispering in disapproval before vanishing into smoke. The villagers say that if you spill oil or waste a flame, you will feel him near — the faint sound of straw brushing stone, a gentle sigh carried by the wind. His punishment is endless, yet his purpose seems transformed: from thief to keeper, from desecrator to guardian.

Artists of the Edo period found quiet fascination in his figure. Unlike the grotesque or flamboyant yokai of the urban imagination, Abura-sumashi is humble, rural, and melancholic. He is the embodiment of an old Japan fading from memory — the world of mountain roads, oil lamps, and whispered superstitions. In painted scrolls he often appears alone, dwarfed by mist and pines, his head heavy as memory itself. His presence in art feels less like fear than nostalgia, a yearning for a time when even small sins carried the weight of eternity.

Children in Kumamoto were once told, "Don't waste the lamp oil, or Abura-sumashi will come for you." The warning lingered long after the lamps turned electric. Yet over generations, he has softened from threat into folklore's quiet conscience. He reminds those who hurry through the dark that every light, however small, must be earned; that reverence for the unseen is what keeps the world balanced.

Sometimes, during still nights when no insects hum and only the fog breathes, villagers swear they see a flicker of movement beside the trail — a glint of wet stone, a straw coat brushing the earth. He never approaches, never fades entirely. He is the echo of an old world's morality, a spirit shaped not by vengeance but by memory — still guarding the sacred oil that once burned for gods and now flickers only in stories.

akaname

nature spirits and elemental forces

filth licker of forgotten baths

In the abandoned bathhouses of old Japan, when the candles sputter and steam turns thick as breath, there are said to dwell creatures who feed not on flesh, but on neglect itself. Akaname, the "filth licker," is one such being — a small, slick-bodied yokai whose presence is a punishment for sloth. Its tongue, long and red as a serpent, laps at the grime of unclean rooms, devouring mold, scum, and human carelessness alike.

The creature's name comes from the words aka (filth or grime) and name (to lick). It was first described in Toriyama Sekien's eighteenth-century scrolls of yokai, where it appears hunched and frog-like, licking the blackened tiles of an abandoned bathhouse. Unlike demons of malice or vengeful ghosts, Akaname exists as a warning: neglect breeds monsters. In homes where the bath was left untended and filth gathered thickly, this spirit was said to slink from the shadows to feed, its wet tongue leaving streaks of clean slime in its wake.

Though small in stature, Akaname's presence chills the air. Witnesses describe it as thin, hair plastered to its skull, its skin forever damp and sticky from the residue it consumes. Its eyes gleam with a feverish hunger — not for sustenance, but for filth itself. It does not harm humans directly; rather, it reveals the harm they do to themselves through laziness. The creature's pleasure lies in what disgusts others, a mirror held up to the darker corners of human habit.

Old mothers in the Edo period invoked its name to frighten children into cleanliness. "Bathe before bed," they warned, "or the Akaname will come lick your dirt instead." The threat was not of death, but of humiliation — to be found wanting by the filth eater, to have one's shame consumed in silence. In this way, Akaname became both household bogeyman and unsung hygiene inspector, patrolling the unseen spaces behind tubs, under floors, and in the corners where dampness blooms.

Some legends suggest the creature was born from the souls of servants who died scrubbing floors or carrying water without thanks. Others claim it is a kami fallen from grace — a minor household deity of purity that turned monstrous when forgotten. In both tales, Akaname represents the same truth: that cleanliness is not mere vanity but spiritual discipline. The bath, to the Japanese mind, is not only for the body but for the soul; to let it rot is to let the spirit decay as well.

Artists of the Meiji and Taishō eras often rendered the creature with grotesque charm. In ukiyo-e prints, it appears mid-lick beside a tub, its tongue stretching across the frame like a red river. The juxtaposition is striking — beauty and filth sharing space, a reminder that art, like morality, must confront what it fears to cleanse it. Later depictions softened it into something almost comical: a household yokai that minds what people forget, more pitiful than frightening, a creature of habit rather than hatred.

Even today, when few bathe in wooden tubs and mildew hides behind polished tile, Akaname lingers in imagination. It has become a symbol of what festers unseen — in houses, in minds, in societies that forget the sacredness of care. The slurping echo in an empty bathroom, the drip that will not stop, the faint slickness beneath the tap — all are reminders that neglect always hungers, and that somewhere, the Filth Licker waits to feed.

azukiarai

nature spirits and elemental forces
bean washer by the stream

There are nights in the Japanese countryside when the sound of flowing water takes on a rhythm that is not the river's own. Between stones, beneath bridges, a soft splashing begins — the unmistakable sound of hands washing something small, followed by a chant whispered half to the night, half to itself:
"Azuki arau zo, shoki shoki."
"I'm washing beans, I'm washing beans.

This is the mark of Azukiarai, the Bean Washer, a yokai of repetition and unease. Neither wholly ghost nor beast, it manifests as sound before shape — an invisible presence whose ritual of washing beans beneath moonlight blurs the line between household labor and haunting. In some villages, it is said to appear as a shadowed old man by the stream; in others, merely a voice, always polite, always unsettlingly close.

Its origins are uncertain. Some scholars trace it to the spirits of servants or peasants who once worked in riverside mills, condemned to relive their endless chores. Others say it is a playful trickster, a creature of mischief that mimics the sounds of the living to lure wanderers near the water's edge. There are tales of travelers following the rhythmic shoki-shoki of beans being washed, only to find the bank empty — until they glance down and see their reflection smiling back when they are not.

The act of washing beans carries sacred resonance in Japan. Azuki beans, with their red hue, are associated with purification and protection from evil. They are boiled during festivals and funerals alike, their steam driving away spirits of misfortune. The irony of Azukiarai's ritual is that it performs an act meant to cleanse, yet does so in eerie solitude, as though trapped in an unfinished prayer. In some regions, villagers whisper that it washes beans to prepare offerings for the dead — a lonely spirit continuing its service beyond life.

Encounters with Azukiarai are often more strange than dangerous. Those who hear its chant are said to be "chosen by coincidence," drawn momentarily into the threshold where the mundane touches the supernatural. If the listener laughs or mocks the sound, the yokai grows angry and splashes water at them, but if one listens in silence, it vanishes peacefully. The true danger lies not in the creature itself, but in distraction — for to follow the sound too far may lead one into deeper waters, where the current erases memory.

In Edo and Meiji-era scrolls, Azukiarai is depicted with an almost comical tenderness: a ragged, wide-eyed creature crouching beside a bucket, its elongated fingers delicately stirring beans like prayer beads. Artists seemed fascinated by its ordinariness — a yokai with no malice, performing the most human of tasks in the loneliest of places. Its figure became a kind of visual koan: a reminder that even in the supernatural world, monotony endures.

Some villagers still claim to hear it near irrigation ditches after heavy rains. When the moonlight gleams red upon the water, the faint clatter of beans can be heard again — rhythmic, patient, eternal. It is not a threat, they say, but a message: that there are spirits in the smallest sounds, that even a simple act like washing beans can echo across worlds.

enenra

nature spirits and elemental forces

spirit of smoke and breath

When the hearth fire dies and the smoke rises in slow spirals toward the eaves, villagers in Japan once whispered that the air itself might awaken. From that drifting veil could emerge Enenra — the smoke spirit — a being of air and memory, formed from the breath of fire. It moves as though dreaming, its body forever dissolving into the sky that birthed it.

Legends say Enenra is born in two ways: from pure flame, as an elemental of wind and ash, or from the spirits of the wicked, whose souls, too light for earth yet too dark for heaven, are reborn as vapor. To see it is to glimpse a boundary between worlds, for Enenra belongs to neither. It lingers in the in-between, a living embodiment of impermanence.

In the Ehon Hyaku Monogatari and other Edo scrolls, the spirit is depicted emerging from a smoky brazier or the smoldering remains of battlefields — a feminine silhouette formed of mist, its hair and robes made entirely of flowing soot. When the smoke moves, her face vanishes; when it pauses, her eyes seem to open for a heartbeat. The artist's brush could never trap her, only suggest her passing. To paint Enenra was to attempt to capture motion itself.

Some describe her as a messenger of transformation — appearing not to harm, but to reveal. When she drifts through rooms where incense burns, she is said to whisper the last thoughts of the departed. When she rises from the bodies of the sinful, her smoke carries the scent of burning regret. In temples, however, her appearance was taken as a sign of purification: a spirit that feeds on corruption and exhales clarity.

Those who encounter her say her movements are mesmerizing. She does not walk or glide but unfolds, her form expanding and contracting like breath itself. When she speaks — if she speaks at all — her voice is the rustle of air through bamboo, intimate yet unreachable. A single word can draw her near; a single exhale can send her away. She is the spirit of transition, of what lingers after the flame's end.

To the philosophers of the Edo era, Enenra represented the soul's subtlety — how identity can persist even in dissolution. Just as incense smoke carries the essence of fragrance long after the stick has burned, so too does the spirit linger in every trace of what it once was. Monks who meditated on her image said she embodied mujo, impermanence: the truth that all things pass, but nothing truly disappears.

In folklore, those pure of heart can see Enenra clearly; the wicked, only as shadow. To glimpse her in full is to understand transience, to witness beauty that exists only while vanishing. For this reason, she is both fear and comfort — a promise that death is not an ending but a transformation as natural as smoke returning to sky.

Even now, when the scent of incense curls through temple corridors or the smoke from cooking fires drifts into twilight, people say she dances there — unseen but present, weaving the unseen stories of the living and the dead. And when smoke trails linger longer than they should, shaping briefly into something almost human, it is said that Enenra has paused for just a moment — to breathe, to remember, and then to fade again into air.

furutsubaki-no-rei

nature spirits and elemental forces
spirit of the ancient camellia

In lonely temple gardens and forgotten graveyards of Japan, the camellia blooms when the air still holds the chill of winter. Its flowers shine like drops of blood upon dark leaves, perfect and silent — and when they fall, they fall whole. To watch one drop is to witness a quiet decapitation, a beauty that ends without warning. From this deathlike grace the Furutsubaki-no-rei, the Spirit of the Old Camellia, is said to rise: a woman of flowers and sorrow, bound forever to the tree that birthed her.

In old tales from Matsue and Kyushu, villagers spoke of ancient camellias that no one dared to cut. The oldest trees — those that had watched centuries of snow and sunlight — were believed to possess souls. When they grew too old, their essence thickened into awareness. From within their trunks, pale women would emerge at twilight, their bodies still streaked with bark, their hair filled with petals. Some called them hanayome no rei, the "bride spirits," for they appeared veiled in beauty yet carried the stillness of death.

Those who encountered one often mistook her for a lost woman wandering among the blossoms. She would bow politely, her movements impossibly gentle. But when she turned, the scent of flowers became cloying — like blood warmed by sunlight — and those who met her gaze too long would grow faint and fall asleep beneath the camellia tree. By morning, they would be found lifeless, a perfect blossom resting on their chest. The villagers said it was the spirit's kiss, or her longing to return the beauty stolen by time.

In some versions, Furutsubaki-no-rei is not malicious, only lonely. She guards the tree from harm, weeping for each petal that falls. The camellia was long considered a noble flower, associated with samurai and the impermanence of life. Yet it also became a symbol of forbidden grief — for just as the flower falls whole, so too did warriors' heads fall on battlefields. To the old spirit, each bloom is a remembrance, each drop a ghost's sigh.

Artists of the Edo period painted her emerging from dark gardens, her skin pale as the moon and her hair flowing like ink down her shoulders. She was neither woman nor ghost, but nature given sorrowful form — a being of beauty too perfect to endure. In these images, camellia petals often fall around her in midair, frozen between blooming and dying, as if the world itself paused in her presence.

Some shrines still hold rituals to appease such spirits. Before cutting a camellia, priests pour water at its roots and whisper apologies, asking its soul not to follow. To harm an old camellia is considered taboo; even today, gardeners hesitate to plant them near graves, for the fallen flower resembles a severed head. In temple courtyards, the oldest trees are left untouched — their blossoms offerings to the dead.

Poets and monks alike saw in Furutsubaki-no-rei the essence of mono no aware — the sorrowful awareness of transience. She is not a creature of vengeance but of memory, haunting those who forget that beauty and mortality share the same stem. Her existence reminds us that nature mourns, too — that the world, in its quiet grace, feels the weight of its own impermanence.

And when spring begins and the first camellia drops without sound, some say she stirs again, brushing the earth with her translucent hand. For one breath of the season, her spirit returns — to stand beneath her ancient tree, to gather fallen blossoms, and to remember, with infinite tenderness, all the things that bloom only to fall.

hiderigami

nature spirits and elemental forces

drought demon

When the wind ceases and the soil begins to break like pottery beneath the sun, the farmers of old Japan would whisper a single name — Hiderigami. It was said that this yokai rode upon the still air of midsummer, a god of drought whose gaze could wither crops and drain rivers with a blink. Wherever it passed, green turned to gray, and even the frogs fell silent beneath the weight of the heat.

The earliest records of Hiderigami appear in the Kojiki and in the scrolls of Konjaku Monogatari, where it is described as a one-eyed, one-armed creature that leaps across the land during the hottest days of the year. Born from the fiery breath of the sun goddess Amaterasu herself, it was once a servant of divine order — a spirit meant to balance abundance with restraint. But when human greed ignored nature's rhythm, Hiderigami turned from guardian to scourge, releasing its terrible hunger upon the world.

Travelers claimed that during the height of summer, if they saw a cloudless horizon that shimmered like glass, it was not the light but the movement of Hiderigami — crawling on invisible winds, its body radiating waves of heat that made the air bend. No weapon could pierce it, for it was not made of flesh but of atmosphere itself. To glimpse its single eye was to feel one's strength evaporate, the moisture in one's breath stolen mid-inhale.

In the Edo period, farmers held rituals to ward it away. At shrines, women would pound rice into flour and scatter it into the air as symbolic "clouds," begging the gods for rain to return. Children carried willow branches dipped in water, waving them skyward to confuse the spirit's sight. When drought lingered too long, priests conducted amagoi ceremonies — rain-invoking prayers that included drawings of Hiderigami burned and cast into wells, the ashes said to call down thunder as penance.

Descriptions of the yokai vary with region. In some provinces, it appears as a gaunt, red-skinned man with one arm and a great lidless eye, leaping from hill to hill. In others, it is a crawling, lizardlike spirit whose scales shine like sunlit mirrors. Scholars of the Meiji era interpreted it as a mythic embodiment of drought itself — an elemental kami whose presence explains the merciless stillness of late summer. Whatever its form, the fear it inspired was universal: the dread of time without water, of heaven withholding its gift.

In certain mountain villages, people whispered that Hiderigami could be appeased by humility. They would pour fresh water over stones, sing to the dry earth, and promise moderation in harvests yet to come. The creature, though monstrous, was still divine in origin — not evil, merely necessary. It reminded mortals that abundance demands balance, that the same sun which ripens rice can just as easily turn it to ash.

Artists often painted Hiderigami in contrast to Amefuri-kozo, the child spirit of rain. In those scrolls, the drought demon crouches low, clawing at dry soil as the rain-child watches from afar with pity. The image captures the eternal cycle: desolation and renewal, heat and water, destruction and rebirth. Together they form the breath of Japan's seasons — the rhythm by which life endures.

hitodama

nature spirits and elemental forces

soul-lights of the dead

On humid summer nights in rural Japan, when the air trembles with the hum of cicadas and the scent of river reeds, people sometimes glimpse small floating fires drifting silently between trees. They move with uncanny calm — not the erratic flicker of flame, but the slow pulse of something alive. These are Hitodama, the "soul balls" of the departed, gentle spirits that rise from the bodies of the dead and wander briefly through the world before finding their way to the other side.

The name Hitodama combines hito (person) and tama (spirit or soul), and their image has haunted Japanese imagination for centuries. In the Konjaku Monogatari and Edo-period ghost scrolls, they appear as pale flames, sometimes blue, sometimes green, sometimes white, hovering at the height of a human heart. They are most often seen near temples, graveyards, and rivers — thresholds between worlds — though travelers have also reported them gliding silently above rice fields, as if tracing the boundaries of forgotten lives.

Ancient belief holds that when a person dies, their soul separates slowly from the body, lingering for a time as light. This luminous form, lighter than air, floats above the corpse, sometimes visible to the living as a faint glow. It is neither ghost nor god, merely the human spirit in transition. The Hitodama's purpose is not to haunt but to move — to drift gently toward peace, guided by unseen currents of wind and memory.

In many folktales, these soul-lights appear to those who mourn too deeply. A widow might see a dim flame near her garden pond and recognize, in its wavering motion, the kindness of her lost husband. A mother might find a pale light lingering at her child's pillow and feel the air grow warm, just for a moment. The Hitodama rarely speak, yet their presence carries understanding beyond words: love that persists even after form has vanished.

Some superstitions warn that to chase a Hitodama is to invite illness, for it draws the curious away from the warmth of life into the cold silence it inhabits. Yet others claim that those who bow their heads and offer a quiet prayer may see the flame brighten — a sign that the spirit has recognized remembrance and will rest more easily. The Hitodama, in this way, teaches the living how to grieve: not with fear, but with respect for the mystery of passing.

Artists of the Edo era painted them with delicate restraint. In ukiyo-e prints, Hitodama appear as floating blue orbs accompanying Yūrei, the long-haired ghosts of human sorrow. But unlike their tormented counterparts, these soul-lights drift peacefully beside them, illuminating darkness rather than deepening it. Poets, too, wrote of them — "small moons that wander between worlds," symbols of transience as lovely as they are unsettling.

The scientific minds of the Meiji period tried to explain them as phosphorescent gas or fireflies, yet even skeptics found beauty in the persistence of the tale. For what the Hitodama represents cannot be measured: the shimmer that remains after loss, the proof that the invisible has weight. Their light reminds people that memory itself glows — not enough to banish night, but enough to keep one from forgetting.

jikininki

nature spirits and elemental forces
corpse-eating spirit of hunger

When dusk settles over mountain temples and the last bells fade into silence, villagers whisper that something stirs near the graves. They do not speak its name loudly, for the Jikininki listens — a creature that feeds on death, drawn to the scent of ritual and the stillness of bodies newly departed. Beneath moonlight, it shuffles toward its feast: a forgotten corpse, a neglected tomb, a place where human reverence has rotted into indifference.

Once, it was human — a monk who lived without compassion, worshipping offerings instead of the souls they were meant to honor. When death came, his body fell to dust, but his hunger did not. It twisted into a curse, binding him to the flesh he once blessed. Now his temple lies empty, and the monk wanders still, searching not for enlightenment but for carrion to quiet the gnawing that never ends.

Witnesses describe the Jikininki as corpse and shadow fused into one: gray skin clinging to bones, a face bloated and collapsing by turns, its eyes burning with a dim, feverish light. When it eats, the world around it trembles slightly — lantern flames bending, wind pausing mid-breath, as though nature itself refuses to watch. What remains after its meal are bones stripped clean and air heavy with the sweet stench of decay.

Some travelers have claimed to see it disguised as an old priest. They speak of stopping at temples during storms, offered shelter by a quiet monk who serves no tea and lights no fire. By morning, the visitor awakens alone, surrounded by upturned graves, their host vanished. Only afterward do they learn the place had been abandoned for generations. The Jikininki, it seems, still remembers the motions of its former life — greeting, bowing, blessing — but all without soul.

There are those who say it does not feed out of pleasure but punishment. Every bite burns its tongue like hot iron; every swallow tears its throat. Yet it cannot stop. In that endless hunger lies its lesson — greed consumes the consumer. Some priests claim that when a Jikininki weeps, the sound is like the crackle of fire on wet wood, as though its tears were trying to extinguish the appetite that damned it.

In Buddhist folklore, it is counted among the gaki, the hungry ghosts, but the Jikininki stands apart — solitary, self-aware, almost human in its shame. Its presence is a mirror to living monks and merchants alike, a reminder that virtue without empathy is as hollow as the belly of a corpse-eater. Where temples fall silent and offerings are taken without prayer, this spirit thrives unseen, keeping count of every sin it once committed.

There is a tale from the north of a wandering priest who performed funeral rites for a poor villager in a remote valley. That night, he stayed in a small hermit's hut and woke to see his host — the kind old monk who had welcomed him — crouched among the graves, tearing at the flesh of the dead. By dawn, the hut was gone, replaced by crumbling stones and the lingering echo of the monk's final cry: "I cannot stop what I have become."

In the modern imagination, Jikininki lingers as one of Japan's most tragic yokai — not born from malice, but from the weight of greed and forgotten devotion. It haunts not only graveyards but hearts, reminding all who worship comfort more than compassion that every offering left untended, every act of kindness withheld, feeds a hunger that never dies.

kappa

nature spirits and elemental forces

watery trickster

Beneath the surface of Japan's tranquil rivers and shaded ponds, something ancient stirs. With skin the color of riverweed and the posture of a crouching child, the Kappa waits—not always with malice, but never without mischief. These aquatic yōkai are among the most iconic in Japanese folklore, revered, feared, and even befriended across generations. Half turtle, half frog, with humanoid features and a shallow bowl of water atop their heads, Kappa are as unpredictable as the currents they inhabit.

The origins of the Kappa are deeply entwined with Japan's relationship to its waterways. References to Kappa appear in Heian-period texts (794–1185) and grew increasingly elaborate in Edo-period ghost stories and travelogues. Their name is composed of "kawa" (river) and "wappa" (child), hinting at their child-sized stature and amphibious habitat. But while their size may seem harmless, the legends surrounding them are anything but. In old tales, they drag livestock—or even people—into the water, their slimy fingers grasping for anything foolish enough to swim alone.

Kappa are usually described as green-skinned, with webbed hands and feet, a beaked mouth, and a turtle-like shell on their back. The most important feature, however, is the depression atop their head, a shallow, water-filled dish. This is the source of their strength, and if the water within it is spilled or dries, the Kappa becomes weak, even immobilized. This vulnerability is the basis for one of the creature's most curious traits—its obsessive politeness. If one bows to a Kappa, it is compelled to return the gesture, thus spilling the water from its head and rendering itself powerless.

Though feared for their drownings and pranks, Kappa are not purely malevolent. They are also known to be keepers of promises, and if treated with respect, can become strange but loyal allies. Farmers have legends of Kappa helping irrigate rice fields, while some tales tell of Kappa teaching bone-setting and healing skills to rural communities. Offerings of cucumbers—especially with one's name carved into them—were historically placed in rivers to appease these beings, as cucumber is said to be their favorite food.

The ambiguity of the Kappa reflects the dual nature of nature itself—capable of both nourishment and danger. Rivers, so essential to life and fertility, also carried the risk of flood, drowning, or disease. Kappa embody this paradox. They are symbols of what lies just beneath the surface—unseen, slippery, and potentially treacherous. They offer a folklore-shaped way to teach children to respect rivers, to be wary of strangers, and to observe traditions that protect both self and community.

Over time, Kappa have swum from the depths of ancient fear into the waters of modern imagination. They appear in manga, anime, festivals, and mascot culture. In spite of their eerie beginnings, their image today is often playful—green, grinning, and cartoonish. Yet behind the friendly face remains the echo of older waters, where a creature neither human nor beast waited patiently for the curious to step too close.

The Kappa endures not because of its fearsome power, but because of its unsettling familiarity. It represents what is just slightly off—a childlike figure with inhuman eyes, a smile that might be friendly or predatory. It reminds us that the world of spirits and yōkai is never far away, only as distant as the next still pool or moss-covered stream.

kawa-uso

nature spirits and elemental forces
river trickster

Where the river bends and the reeds sigh in twilight, there comes laughter — high and bright, almost human, almost kind. Fishermen who linger too long along the banks of Japan's quieter streams know that sound well. It belongs to the Kawa-uso, the river otter yokai, whose mischief ripples just beneath the surface of calm water. To some, it's a playful guardian of the rivers; to others, a deceiver who mimics human voice and shape with unnerving ease.

In the oldest tales, Kawa-uso began as ordinary otters, creatures admired for their intelligence and curiosity. But when they grew too clever, too fond of human company, they crossed the veil between animal and spirit. The river blessed them with the gift of transformation — and with it, the curse of loneliness. Now they dwell in half-seen places: beneath bridges, inside fog, laughing at travelers who mistake that sound for a child's giggle or a friend's familiar call.

Those who claim to have seen one say it first appears as a small otter, gliding through the shallows with harmless grace. Yet when moonlight strikes the water, its form lengthens — fur blending into skin, paws stretching into fingers. It emerges as a beautiful youth with damp hair and a glimmering smile, beckoning from the edge of the current. Many have followed such figures, thinking them lost villagers or lovers returned from war, only to vanish into the black mouth of the river.

Not all Kawa-uso are cruel. In some regions, they trade gifts with fishermen — silver fish for offerings of sake left by the water's edge. There are stories of them rescuing drowning children, carrying them ashore before disappearing in a splash. Yet their moods change with the current: gentle when the water is calm, violent when it floods. Their laughter, when heard near storm-swollen rivers, is considered a warning. It means the river will take what it's owed.

One legend from Tottori speaks of a Kawa-uso that wore the faces of its victims. It would kill a traveler by the river, peel away his likeness, and wear it like a mask to trick others into trust. Only when it laughed — that hollow, bubbling sound — did the truth show through. The villagers caught it one dawn and found beneath the human skin nothing but teeth, eyes, and fur. They buried it by the reeds, but its laughter still echoed whenever fog rose thick on the water.

In art, Kawa-uso appear sleek and ambiguous: creatures caught mid-shift, neither beast nor man. Scroll painters of the Edo period often rendered them with wide, knowing eyes — a balance between innocence and cruelty. Their image became a parable for desire itself, for the way beauty can draw you closer even as it drowns you. To watch a Kawa-uso swim is to see temptation made liquid.

There's a saying in riverside villages: "Beware the one who laughs by water." It might be a child at play, or it might be something older, wearing a child's joy like a mask. Yet for all their danger, the Kawa-uso remain strangely beloved — a reflection of humankind's own duality. Like the rivers they haunt, they are life-givers and destroyers, guides and deceivers.

And sometimes, when night hangs still and the water gleams silver beneath the stars, you might glimpse movement where none should be — the sleek arch of a furred back, a ripple that becomes a smile. Listen closely. The laughter that follows isn't meant to scare you. It's just the river remembering your voice.

kodama

nature spirits and elemental forces

echoing spirits of the sacred trees

In the hushed heart of Japan's forests, where cedar trunks rise like pillars and sunlight filters through in trembling shafts, the air sometimes carries a second voice — a faint echo that repeats your own words a heartbeat too late. Locals say it isn't the mountain answering, but a spirit listening. These are the Kodama, the souls of ancient trees, guardians of the forest's breath, invisible until the living forget to tread lightly.

The word Kodama means "tree spirit" or "echo," and in Japan's oldest tales, it refers both to the sound that replies from deep woods and to the invisible beings who make it. When a tree has lived for centuries, its roots drinking from the same spring generation after generation, it is said to awaken — its essence ripening into sentience. Not every tree holds a Kodama, but those that do are sacred. To cut one is to cut the spirit that sustains the mountain itself.

Travelers once marked such trees with white paper cords called shimenawa, the same used to sanctify shrines. At night, villagers swore they could see lights moving softly between the trunks — not fireflies, but Kodama gliding from tree to tree, whispering in tones too old to understand. If a woodsman's axe struck the wrong bark, a mournful cry would echo through the forest, and his hand would wither before the moon waned. Thus, people learned reverence not from scripture, but from silence.

There is a story from Aomori of a lumberjack who ignored the elders' warning and felled a massive cedar said to house a Kodama. The instant the trunk split, blood gushed from the wood, staining the soil. That night, the man's house shook with the groaning of timber and the sound of wind that spoke in words he could not bear to hear. By morning, every tool in his shed had rusted to dust. The villagers built a small shrine where the cedar once stood, leaving offerings of rice and clear water to calm the spirit's grief.

In other regions, the Kodama is less wrathful — shy, almost playful. Travelers who lose their way sometimes follow the sound of faint laughter or the tapping of small feet, only to find themselves at the edge of a stream, the path restored. Children who wander too deep into the woods return saying they met little glowing people who vanished when thanked. These tales breathe the gentler truth: the Kodama are not guardians of punishment, but protectors of balance, reminding mortals that the forest has eyes and ears.

Art from the Heian and Edo periods portrays them as ethereal, childlike beings or small globes of light drifting through groves of cedar and cypress. In Buddhist interpretation, they are considered mujō no rei — transient spirits that reflect life's impermanence. Trees, after all, live longer than men but not forever; the Kodama carries that patient awareness. Its song, the echo, is not mimicry but memory — the forest remembering your voice, then returning it so you might hear yourself anew.

Rituals to honor them still linger in rural Japan. Villagers pour the first cup of sake at the base of old trees, clap twice softly, and listen for an answer. In spring, the sound of wind through leaves is said to be the Kodama stirring, their laughter hidden in the rustle. Those who listen with humility claim the echo becomes music — proof that nature is not silent, only waiting for someone to hear it.

mokumokuren

nature spirits and elemental forces

eyes that dwell in torn shoji

There is a peculiar fear found not in the dark itself, but in the moment you realize the dark is looking back. Old houses in Japan carry such silences. Beneath their sagging roofs and brittle walls, paper screens flutter with drafts and whispers. When the holes in those screens begin to blink, the Mokumokuren has awakened.

Its name means "many eyes," and that is all it is — a legion of gazes blooming like fungi in the wounds of forgotten paper. It lives where neglect gathers: in guest rooms long unvisited, inns left to dust, temples where prayers have stopped. To tear a shoji and leave it unrepaired is to invite the world of spirits inside, for the Mokumokuren slips through those small absences and fills them with its sight.

Some travelers describe entering abandoned inns at night and feeling the peculiar weight of attention. When they light a lantern, the room reveals itself as ordinary — until a glimmer catches in the corner of torn paper. Dozens of eyes watch from the walls, reflecting the flame. Some are curious, others weary, and some seem almost sad, as if remembering what it was like to be unseen.

One folktale tells of a merchant who slept in such a ruined inn. Waking at midnight, he felt his hair prickle as he realized the walls were breathing. Eyes stared from every tear in the paper, and as he watched, they began to turn toward him, one by one. Terrified, he stabbed at the nearest with his chopsticks — only to find them sticky with his own blood when dawn came. He left at sunrise, certain the Mokumokuren had borrowed his vision for the night.

Other stories claim that these eyes are not malevolent but mournful. Each one, it is said, belongs to a forgotten spirit, the echo of someone who once lived within the house — servants, guests, children. Their memories linger, unable to sleep, so they peer through the holes hoping to see life return. When a home is repaired, when light fills the rooms once more, the eyes close gently and vanish into dust.

In Buddhist interpretation, the Mokumokuren embodies kan, awareness without attachment. It is the watcher of the watcher — the soul that sees yet cannot act. Artists of the Edo period loved to paint it for this reason: a symbol of conscience, of the way every neglect, every absence, eventually grows eyes. It became a quiet warning to householders — mend what is broken, or the unseen will learn to look.

When wind passes through old homes in rural Japan and the paper screens rustle without cause, some people still lower their voices. They say the Mokumokuren are stirring, opening their eyelids to glimpse the living for a moment before closing again. It's a soundless exchange between two worlds — human care and spirit curiosity — as fragile as the paper that separates them.

To live in harmony with them requires no exorcism, only mindfulness. Replace what is torn, sweep what gathers dust, and remember that even silence has witnesses. For every wall, every doorway, every neglected corner might one day blink awake — and you will know then that you were never alone, not even in the stillness of your own home.

namazu

nature spirits and elemental forces

great earthshaker´s catfish

Beneath the islands of Japan, where rivers meet veins of molten rock and the roots of mountains twist like sleeping dragons, lies a catfish too vast to measure. Its name is Namazu, the Earthshaker. Each time it moves its tail, the ground trembles; when it thrashes, cities fall. Yet it does not stir from malice but from instinct — the heartbeat of the planet made flesh.

The myth of Namazu emerges from the Edo period, a time when earthquakes scarred the land and belief sought meaning in disaster. People imagined that Japan floated upon the back of this mighty fish, restrained only by the god Kashima, who pinned it down with a great stone called the kaname-ishi. When the god's vigilance faltered — when prayers waned, or human greed grew too loud — Namazu shifted restlessly, and the earth answered with fury.

Fishermen along the eastern coast swore that before great tremors, the water would change: clear one moment, dark the next, as though something enormous stirred far below. Sometimes they found catfish leaping in panic before an earthquake struck — smaller echoes of their divine ancestor. The people read these signs as warnings: the spirit of Namazu was awakening, and the land would pay for its imbalance.

After the catastrophic Edo earthquake of 1855, the image of Namazu flooded Japanese art. Woodblock prints known as namazu-e portrayed the giant fish crushed by Kashima's stone, or laughing as it broke free to punish corrupt officials. In some, the yokai smiled while distributing gold coins to commoners — a subtle irony: destruction as social justice, the quaking of the earth as divine reordering. The people began to see Namazu not only as a monster, but as a bringer of renewal.

In certain versions, the catfish even speaks. It rumbles through the soil with a voice like thunder, lamenting that humans build too greedily and take too much. "When I move," it says, "you remember balance." Thus, the earthquakes became a kind of grim compassion — nature's reminder that power cannot be hoarded without consequence. The Namazu was not evil; it was the conscience of the land, rising when harmony was forgotten.
Rituals soon followed to calm the spirit. In temples dedicated to Kashima, priests prayed over catfish-shaped charms carved from wood or copper. Farmers placed them near wells and rice paddies to appease the beast that slept below. These Namazu omamori became both talismans of protection and acknowledgments of fear — tokens of gratitude to the creature that bore the islands on its back, yet could crush them in its dreams.

To artists and poets, Namazu became an emblem of renewal through chaos. Its movements erased arrogance, leveled the towers of the proud, and fed the earth with new beginnings. In its deep, unknowable body, they saw the spirit of Japan itself: resilient, ever-shifting, shaped by destruction yet never destroyed.

And so, when tremors ripple through the land even now, some still whisper thanks before they pray. The ground quakes, the lamps sway, and somewhere in the dark waters beneath the world, the great Namazu turns over once more — restless, vast, and dreaming of balance.

nurarihyon

nature spirits and elemental forces

master of the house

In the shadowed corners of Japanese yōkai tradition, there exists a figure whose menace is not in violence or horror, but in intrusion. Nurarihyon is an enigma cloaked in calm; an old man with a gourd-shaped head, dressed like an aristocrat, who slips unnoticed into homes and proceeds to act like he owns them. No locked door deters him, no family seems to question his presence. He pours tea, settles in like an honored guest, and vanishes just as quietly as he arrived—leaving behind only unease and mystery.

The first written references to Nurarihyon appear in Edo-period yōkai picture scrolls, such as the Hyakkai Zukan (1737) by Sawaki Suushi. Though many yōkai are wild or monstrous, Nurarihyon is distinctly refined. He wears the robes of a kanrei or noble, complete with obi sashes and layered silk. His name combines nureru ("to slip in" or "to soak") and hyoron, a reference to his elongated, gourd-like head, which resembles the hyotan gourd. This odd yet unmistakable silhouette makes him easy to recognize—if only one notices before he vanishes.

Unlike creatures who roam the forests or haunt remote shrines, Nurarihyon is most at home in urban or domestic settings. He appears in kitchens, tea rooms, and entrances of homes, usually in the evening when families are preoccupied. In many stories, he behaves with such calm confidence that homeowners are unsure whether he's a forgotten guest, a distant relative, or someone of importance they failed to remember. His magic lies in social ambiguity, in the cultural instinct not to question someone who carries themselves with authority.

Over time, Nurarihyon's myth evolved beyond that of a simple intruder. In modern adaptations, especially manga and folklore reinterpretations, he is sometimes described as the leader of all yōkai—a quiet puppet master of the supernatural world. This portrayal adds depth to his legend: no longer a mere parasite, but a being of great intelligence who governs the unseen with patience and subtlety. He does not command through fear, but through infiltration, suggestion, and presence—a master not just of the house, but of perception itself.

In art, Nurarihyon is almost always shown sipping tea or entering a room, his posture relaxed, his expression mild. Unlike demons or spirits of vengeance, he offers no direct threat, yet those who encounter him often feel unsettled afterward. Something was out of place, something ancient had entered the home, and somehow everyone let it happen. He reveals how supernatural disturbance can exist in the calmest of moments, how the uncanny doesn't always scream—it sometimes sips tea.

The essence of Nurarihyon is quiet disruption. He doesn't break the rules; he rewrites them with subtle gestures. He is the stranger who knows where the cups are kept, the ghost who never rattles chains. In the pantheon of Japanese spirits, he stands apart—not by strength or terror, but by grace, suggestion, and the lingering discomfort of a presence you couldn't quite explain.

raijū

nature spirits and elemental forces
thunder beast of the storm god

The first crack of thunder over the summer plains was once said to be the roar of Raijū, the storm beast, hurling itself across the sky. Farmers who looked up during lightning storms swore they saw flashes of shape — fur, claws, eyes — woven into the light itself. To witness it was to feel the divine made visible for a heartbeat, before it vanished again into cloud and rumble.

The name Raijū means "thunder animal," and in ancient scrolls it appears as a companion of Raijin, the god who beats his drums to make thunder roll. But Raijū is more than a pet — it is thunder's living essence, the fierce spark that gives the sky its voice. Sometimes it descends to earth when storms break open the heavens, curling into trees, mountains, or even sleeping humans, drawn by the rhythm of their hearts.

In one Edo legend, a farmer napping beneath a tree awoke to find his belly opened by a lightning strike — yet no wound remained. Villagers said Raijū had leapt into his body to hide from Raijin's wrath. When the god called, it burst out again in a flash of blue fire. From that day, no one in the village dared to sleep under open skies during storms; it was said the thunder beast hunted warm bodies to rest within until the rain ceased.

Though often imagined as a wolf or cat woven of lightning, Raijū is a shapeshifter by nature. Some tales describe it as a glowing serpent twisting through thunderclouds; others, as a weasel or ferret that skitters along the wind. In every form, it is restless, untamed, and radiant — a living current. When it strikes the ground, the air smells of ozone and burning cedar, and all who see it feel their skin rise with static, as though the sky itself had touched them.

In Shinto belief, lightning was both terror and blessing — a divine force that scorched, purified, and renewed. When Raijū struck the earth, people saw not destruction but fertility, for the lightning fed the fields with heavenly fire. Farmers left offerings of rice and sake at charred trees where lightning had fallen, believing the beast had touched the world to mark it sacred. The burned trunks were never cut down; they stood as shrines to the storm.

Artists of the Edo and Meiji periods adored Raijū's fluid form. In paintings and netsuke carvings, it blazes like a comet caught mid-roar, fur rendered as flame, eyes alive with light. Poets compared it to "a god's thought in motion," and storytellers claimed its cry could split the heart of arrogance. Every flash of lightning, they said, was Raijū turning in its sleep — a reminder that the world's order depends on energy that refuses to be still.

One quiet superstition lingers from those times: that people struck by lightning are not cursed but chosen. Their survival marks them as touched by Raijū — alive because they carried the thunder's heart and endured it. Such souls were thought to walk with heightened purpose, forever followed by storms that recognized them as kin.

And so the Raijū endures, as wild and glorious as the sky that births it. Each bolt of lightning, each rumble of thunder, each pulse of electric light across the horizon is its fleeting signature — a beast of divine fury, vanishing before it can be understood. For in truth, Raijū is not a creature to be seen, but a presence to be felt, racing through every storm that dares to remember its name.

suiko

nature spirits and elemental forces

river corpse demon

The water looks calm before it takes you. Beneath the surface, between mud and reflection, something ancient waits — its pulse matching the slow current, its patience endless. This is the Suiko, the water corpse demon, feared by fishermen and travelers for centuries. It is said to drag victims into rivers without a splash, leaving only ripples where their names once were.

The word Suiko (水虎) means "water tiger," though few who see it live long enough to describe it as feline. It's a cousin to the Kappa, yet darker and older — a creature of stagnation rather than flow. While the playful Kappa delights in mischief and riddles, the Suiko feeds purely on blood. Where it dwells, fish die and the water takes on a sweet, rotting scent. Its favorite haunts are deep, quiet pools where no wind reaches and no frogs sing.

Villagers in Kyushu and Chūgoku once claimed to find bodies pulled from rivers with a perfect round hole in the chest. The heart and liver would be missing, yet the skin unbroken elsewhere. "The Suiko took them," they said. "It drained their souls through that single wound." Unlike its cousin, the Suiko shows no interest in games or courtesy. It kills with the efficiency of nature itself — silent, inevitable, unfeeling.

A few brave priests have claimed to exorcise them. They say the creature's power lies in the water atop its head, held within a shallow bowl like that of a Kappa. Spill or dry it, and the demon weakens. Yet the Suiko is cunning — its pool never empties, for it feeds on blood to replenish it. In some tales, it can even shape-shift into a drowned victim to lure others closer, its skin cool and damp as river stones.

Edo-period storytellers whispered of a samurai who fought a Suiko by moonlight after it stole his horse. When he struck it, his blade passed through water itself. The creature smiled, crimson leaking from its grin, and vanished beneath the surface, leaving the samurai's reflection trembling. By morning, the pond had dried — only mud remained, and the smell of iron. They built a shrine there, hoping the river god would forgive what slept below.

Artists painted Suiko with elegance and menace intertwined — sleek limbs, dripping moss, eyes like copper coins in darkness. It fascinated Edo's urban imagination: a monster that mirrored the city's new fears of progress and pollution. The still waters that once nourished life now hid corruption; the Suiko became its symbol, a creature born from beauty turned rotten.

Though few claim to see them now, some rivers in Japan still carry offerings of sake poured quietly from the shore — not to honor, but to appease. When a fisherman's line tugs too sharply, when a swimmer vanishes without trace, elders murmur, "The Suiko has fed." They do not shout or curse. They bow, because they understand: every current hides a hunger, every reflection watches back.

And if, one evening, you lean too close to a mirror-smooth river and see a shape rise beneath your own — glowing eyes, a ripple, a hand reaching from below — it's already too late. The Suiko has chosen you, and the water will close over your breath as quietly as silk falling shut.

tsuchigumo

nature spirits and elemental forces
subterranean spider-demons

Long before the samurai ruled and the capital glittered in Heian light, Japan was a landscape of shadows and hidden tribes. In those earliest centuries, before the empire had spread its reach across the mountains, whispers told of monstrous beings that refused to kneel to the emperor's divine lineage. They were called Tsuchigumo — "earth spiders." Part spirit, part human, part beast, they lived in caverns and forests, building webs as vast as valleys and waging silent war against the throne.

The name itself was born as insult. The Yamato court used it to brand outsiders — rebels, mountain people, and those who resisted assimilation — as inhuman. Yet myth took root where politics began. Over time, these exiled tribes became literalized into monsters: vast spider-demons lurking underground, their limbs reaching up to ensnare the civilized world. The Tsuchigumo thus transformed from metaphor into myth — an embodiment of Japan's buried defiance.

By the Heian period, stories of Tsuchigumo were entwined with the legends of heroism. Scrolls recount how the warrior Minamoto no Raikō and his loyal retainers hunted a Tsuchigumo that had haunted Kyoto's outskirts, disguising itself as a wounded monk. When Raikō struck the apparition with his sword, the creature's illusion shattered — blood sprayed like rain, and from the monk's robes spilled a thousand spider legs. Following the trail into a dark cave, Raikō found a web as large as a temple, filled with corpses of soldiers who had vanished over the years.

In some versions, when Raikō pierced the spider's heart, its dying breath released swarms of ghostly heads — the spirits of those who had opposed the imperial army centuries before. The tale was retold endlessly, evolving from a heroic victory into an act of exorcism: the slaying of chaos, the triumph of centralized order over the wild, forgotten gods of the earth. Yet the Tsuchigumo never truly died. It merely retreated deeper, beneath the soil of every story.

Edo-era artists painted Tsuchigumo with both terror and reverence. Some depicted it as a hulking arachnid with the face of a noblewoman, weaving illusions to protect her hidden village. Others showed it as a skeletal monster wrapped in clouds of silk, its gaze mournful rather than cruel. To them, Tsuchigumo symbolized something more complex than evil — the spirit of those crushed by history, the conscience of a nation that grew from conquest.

Scholars later saw in it the memory of ancient indigenous peoples, perhaps the Kumaso or Emishi, labeled monsters to justify their destruction. Its story, then, is not only supernatural but human: the victors' myth carved into the flesh of the defeated. Every web it spins ties past to present — every thread a name forgotten by the light.

When storms pass through mountain valleys, villagers still point toward caves where no wind stirs and say, "That is where the Earth Spider sleeps." Offerings of sake and rice are left near cave mouths, not in fear, but in apology. For the Tsuchigumo's tale reminds them that the ground beneath their feet once belonged to others — and that no empire, no matter how divine, can erase what the earth remembers.

At night, when mist drifts through cedar roots and the soil seems to breathe, it is said you can hear faint whispering, like silk being drawn through wood. That is the Tsuchigumo dreaming — weaving again, endlessly, the story that once wove it into myth.

bake-neko

shapeshifters, tricksters and illusions
shape-shifting cat

The old people say a cat that lives too long begins to dream differently. It watches its masters from the rafters, learns their habits, mimics their sighs. When the household grows careless, when prayers stop and lamps burn low, the cat rises on its hind legs and walks like a shadow pretending to be human. That is the birth of the Bake-neko — the "changing cat," born from familiarity, patience, and quiet resentment.

Legends trace it to Edo-period streets, where cats prowled sake shops and bathhouses, their eyes catching lamplight like coins. A cat fed on human affection for too many years was said to gather a spirit within its belly. On the night of its awakening, its tail split in two, fire danced at its tips, and its voice grew clear enough to curse. From that moment, it was no longer a pet but a mirror of the home that made it.

Some Bake-neko were gentle, protecting the households that once cherished them. They kept vermin and ill fortune away, curling by the hearth while their twin-tailed silhouettes flickered on the wall. Others turned vengeful — especially those killed unjustly. In those stories, the murdered cat returns upright and robed like a woman, knocking at the door it once guarded. Its yellow eyes shine with recognition, and its smile shows too many teeth.

One tale from Saga Prefecture tells of a merchant who drowned his wife's beloved cat out of jealousy. Days later, the wife fell sick; each night she dreamed of her pet whispering beside her futon. When the merchant found claw marks across his chest, the villagers said he had been "visited." They burned incense and begged forgiveness, but the Bake-neko had already taken its revenge — the merchant's reflection no longer showed his own face.

The creature's powers are many: it can speak human language, grow to the size of a tiger, or breathe ghost-fire that dances in pale rings. Some take the form of their mistresses, serving tea to guests who never realize they are sipping beside a cat's illusion. Others haunt teahouses and theaters, drawn to music and gossip, their tails hidden beneath silken robes. Wherever laughter and vanity gather, the Bake-neko listens, remembering every secret.

To the scholars of Edo, this yokai symbolized the uncanny domestic — the idea that the familiar world might revolt. The cat, long a symbol of femininity and mystery, reflected anxieties about servants, wives, and the private spaces men assumed they controlled. Yet beneath the fear was admiration: the Bake-neko was clever, graceful, indomitable — everything a creature of spirit ought to be.

Even now, storytellers say that when a cat sits before a shrine and stares too long at the flame, something within the light stares back. If it bows its head three times before leaving, that house will soon hear footsteps at night — soft, padded, and deliberate. But do not drive it away. Leave a bowl of sake and a kind word, for not all watchers are enemies. Some merely wish to be remembered.

And so the Bake-neko prowls on, both ghost and guardian, purring in the threshold between affection and fear. The house that keeps its hearth clean and its hearts honest has nothing to dread. But if cruelty has lived there — if betrayal lingers unspoken — then the next flicker of candlelight may reveal a pair of golden eyes, smiling from the shadows, waiting to settle an old, forgotten debt.

futa-kuchi-onna

shapeshifters, tricksters and illusions

woman with two mouths

On quiet nights when the air is heavy and the candlelight flickers like a heartbeat, villagers whisper of women who never seem to eat. Their skin remains fair, their bodies strong, and yet no one ever sees them lift chopsticks to their lips. Some laugh it off as vanity; others watch the rice bowls emptying by morning and wonder what feeds them in secret. And then, one evening, someone glimpses a ripple beneath the hair — a second mouth, hidden at the back of the head, opening wide in the dark. Thus begins the tale of the Futa-kuchi-onna, the woman cursed with two mouths: one delicate and silent, the other voracious and cruel.

The first of her kind is said to have been born in a household ruled by miserliness. Her husband, a stingy merchant, rejoiced that his wife ate so little, calling her the perfect woman — obedient, thrifty, uncomplaining. But each morning, his storerooms grew lighter, his rice dwindled, his pickled fish gone. One night he crept near and saw her hair twist apart like black serpents, feeding a hidden mouth that laughed behind her. The second mouth spoke in a rasping voice, mocking him, demanding more food, its tongue lashing like flame. In terror and shame, he realized the mouth was not a monster — it was the voice of his own greed, feeding on everything he had once hoarded.

Not all tales begin with avarice. Some say the yokai arises when guilt festers in silence. A woman who starved her stepchild might awaken one morning to find pain biting through her skull. Days later, a mouth bursts open at the wound, eternally screaming for sustenance — the spirit of the dead child gnawing from within. In these darker versions, the Futa-kuchi-onna is not born but made, her second mouth an unrelenting echo of conscience. It laughs when she smiles, weeps when she sleeps, and demands offerings no shrine can satisfy.

In the old provinces of Tōhoku and Niigata, travelers swore they heard laughter rising from the hills — the laughter of hair combs snapping in half as the yokai's living hair tangled itself into knots. Those who fed her second mouth were spared; those who mocked her beauty lost their own. Mothers left offerings of steamed rice on altars for her spirit, hoping to keep her hunger from falling upon their daughters. The whisper spread that even the gods of hunger bowed before her, for she bore hunger made flesh.

Artists and storytellers of the Edo period painted her not merely as horror, but as tragedy. In ukiyo-e scrolls, she gazes demurely over her shoulder while the monstrous mouth yawns open behind her, capturing the eternal tension between what is seen and what is silenced. The brushwork emphasized contrast — front serenity, back chaos — a metaphor for the hidden suffering within social obedience. The yokai's dual mouths became a symbol for women's silenced voices in an era that prized submission: the hunger for truth devouring the self from behind.

As her story spread through theater and print, interpretations multiplied. Some said the curse struck those who denied themselves pleasure, repressing hunger and emotion until it turned inward and demanded release. Others believed the Futa-kuchi-onna was a guardian spirit of balance — consuming what humans wasted, punishing gluttony and deprivation alike. In this reading, she was not a demon but a teacher, reminding mortals that neglecting the body or the heart invites ruin.

hannya

shapeshifters, tricksters and illusions
mask of jealousy

Long before the sound of temple bells faded from the night, there were stories whispered about women whose love burned too fiercely for the mortal world. They were said to be consumed by passion so deep that their hearts melted into venom, their beauty warped by jealousy, and their souls twisted until they became Hannya — demons born not of evil, but of unbearable emotion. Her name echoes through Noh theater and folklore alike, her face both alluring and terrifying, her tears still wet beneath the mask.

In its earliest form, Hannya was not merely a demon, but a woman wronged — a lover betrayed, a wife abandoned, or a nun who fell from grace after her heart turned against her vows. The transformation begins quietly: love curdles into suspicion, and suspicion ferments into rage. Her breath grows hot, her reflection distorts, and horns pierce her brow like accusations taking shape. When the final shreds of humanity fall away, the Hannya stands revealed — part woman, part monster, her beauty preserved like glass over rotting despair.

The mask of Hannya first appeared in Noh theater during Japan's Muromachi period (14th–16th century), carved by artisans who understood the fragile tension between fury and heartbreak. When viewed straight on, the mask appears furious; when tilted downward, it weeps. This duality was no accident — it captured the very essence of human contradiction: that hatred and sorrow often share the same face. Each flicker of torchlight across her horns made her story tremble between vengeance and tragedy.

Beneath the performance, however, lived the myth itself. Some said a woman became Hannya after being consumed by envy — her heart ignited by betrayal so deep it summoned demonic fire. Others claimed she was cursed by the gods to reflect the consequence of human obsession, her transformation a warning to all who cling too tightly to what must be released. In Buddhist interpretations, the Hannya is the embodiment of the Three Poisons — desire, anger, and ignorance — consuming the soul like an eternal flame.

Yet there are tales that grant her mercy. In some, the Hannya regains her humanity at the moment she recognizes her own reflection. Seeing herself as a demon, she wails in grief so pure that the curse shatters. Her horns dissolve, her fangs dull, and she vanishes into mist — her redemption born from self-awareness. This motif resonated with the Buddhist idea of release through understanding, turning the horror of Hannya into a mirror for enlightenment. The lesson whispered through the centuries: the true hell is the one we make within ourselves.

In villages and temples, her story took on protective meaning. Hannya masks were hung above doors to ward off spirits, as though her wrath, once unleashed, could now guard against lesser evils. Travelers carried amulets engraved with her face to keep away betrayal and misfortune, believing the demon's suffering would consume any approaching curse. Thus the once-feared woman became an inverted guardian — a being whose pain shielded others from pain.

Ukiyo-e masters painted her with both tenderness and dread: tears glinting on monstrous cheeks, fire reflected in eyes that once knew love. She was not a fiend, they insisted, but a portrait of emotion itself — a reminder that love, if left to fester, devours the very thing it seeks to protect. Her story traveled beyond temple walls, becoming an emblem of beauty's ruin and the sacred danger of desire.

hone-onna

shapeshifters, tricksters and illusions

bone woman of lingering love

There are nights in northern Japan when a soft knock comes at the door and an old lover's voice calls from the darkness. Those who dare to answer see a woman standing there — pale, graceful, her lantern glowing faintly through the fog. Her scent is of camellias, her eyes full of warmth, and her smile as tender as ever. But by dawn, the neighbors find only bones in the bed, for the visitor was no living woman at all. She was Hone-onna, the Bone Woman, a revenant whose love endures long after her flesh has turned to dust.

In Edo-period ghost tales, Hone-onna is said to rise from her grave driven by passion so deep that even death cannot sever it. She visits the man she loved in life, appearing as she once was — young, beautiful, and gentle. To him, the illusion is perfect: her skin warm, her laughter soft, her presence intoxicating. Yet when light falls upon her, her beauty collapses into horror — a skeleton still draped in the remnants of her burial robe, clinging to her lover with bony fingers. She embodies the terrible persistence of human desire: love that will not die, even when the body has.

Some stories tell of a man who, blinded by longing, welcomes her each night, never questioning her chill touch or the way her lantern burns without smoke. His neighbors, hearing strange noises, peep inside and see him entwined with a skeleton, its skull resting against his chest. When they intervene, he dies instantly — his life consumed by the embrace of his ghostly bride. From such tales came the belief that Hone-onna feeds not on flesh but on affection itself, draining vitality from those unable to release the past.

Other legends place her among the yūrei, the wandering dead who linger because of unfulfilled emotion. In this view, Hone-onna is not malevolent but trapped, repeating her love as a ritual of mourning. The lamp she carries symbolizes both devotion and delusion — a flame that refuses to die out, flickering with every heartbeat of memory. The living who see her light at night are warned not to follow, for to do so is to walk willingly into one's own grave.

In the old kabuki and ukiyo-e prints, artists portrayed Hone-onna as a paradox of grace and horror. Her beauty gleams in candlelight, yet the faint outline of bone beneath her skin betrays her nature. The audience was meant to feel both pity and dread, to recognize how love, unchecked by wisdom, can transform into something eternal and destructive. She was not merely a ghost but a mirror to grief itself — the way longing can rot even the purest affection when it clings too tightly to what is lost.

In Buddhist interpretation, her tale reflects mujō, the impermanence of all things. To cling to love beyond its natural span is to defy the cycle of rebirth. Thus, Hone-onna's haunting becomes a parable of release — to let go, or to become the ghost of one's own obsession. Priests in rural temples performed rites to calm such spirits, chanting sutras and placing lanterns by riverbanks to guide them toward peace. Yet still, people whispered that some lights refused to drift downstream, flickering endlessly at the edge of the water, waiting for the one they once loved

Each version reimagines her differently: a warning against desire, a symbol of loyalty beyond death, or a victim of time itself. Yet the essence remains unchanged. The Hone-onna walks wherever love refuses to yield, her lantern aglow with memory, her footsteps light as falling ash.

ittan-momen

shapeshifters, tricksters and illusions

drifting cloth of night

There are stories whispered in the dark fields of Kagoshima, of a simple bolt of cotton that takes flight after sunset. It moves without sound, gliding through the air like a ribbon of moonlight. Farmers returning from the fields, travelers crossing quiet paths, or children staring into the dusk have seen it drifting low — a long strip of white fabric twisting in the wind, searching. They call it Ittan-momen, the one-tan cotton, a yokai so unassuming that its terror lies in its simplicity.

Few creatures capture the Japanese imagination of animism as perfectly as this one. Born from the spirit of a forgotten cloth roll, neglected in an old weaving shop or blown from a loom by an autumn storm, the Ittan-momen is proof that even the most ordinary thing may awaken with a soul. Some say it becomes alive after absorbing the loneliness of its maker, the breath of the spinner trapped in its threads. Others claim it is a fragment of a burial shroud caught by the wind, a piece of the dead made restless. Whatever its origin, it soars with eerie grace, a spirit neither fully alive nor entirely ghost.

Those unlucky enough to cross its path learn its true nature. The Ittan-momen does not simply drift — it descends. With a flick of its long body, it wraps around a victim's face or neck, tightening like a snake. Its touch is soft as silk but cold as death. The more one struggles, the more it constricts, smothering breath and light until all falls silent. Villagers once said that its victims died without a sound, their mouths filled with cloth and their eyes open to the empty sky. At dawn, the fabric vanished again, leaving no trace but a faint scent of cotton in the morning air.

Yet not all tales paint the creature as malicious. In some remote regions of Kyushu, people speak of Ittan-momen as a curious being, mischievous rather than murderous. It may wrap around travelers only to startle them, or brush gently against the skin before darting away like a gust of wind. Old weavers used to bow to the wind before starting work, murmuring a prayer: "May my cloth never fly without my will." To them, the Ittan-momen symbolized the fine line between art and danger — the spirit that dwells in every handmade thing, waiting to be remembered.

In Edo-period paintings, the yokai is often portrayed floating above bamboo groves or temples, its length rippling through indigo skies. Unlike monstrous demons or grotesque ghosts, its form is abstract and graceful, embodying the beauty of movement itself. Artists saw it as a metaphor for fleeting existence — a thing of use becoming a thing of freedom, a product of human hands escaping their control. In this sense, the Ittan-momen carries both fear and liberation, an image of what happens when creation itself refuses to stay bound.

There is a quiet poetry in its legend. The creature's name — "one roll of cotton" — evokes domestic life, the hum of the spinning wheel, the warmth of fabric against skin. Yet the same material becomes deadly in the wind, a reminder that everything made by humans may one day turn against them if neglected or forgotten. The yokai's flight through the night is both warning and elegy, an expression of the Shinto belief that every object has a kami, a spirit, deserving of respect.

Children are told to hurry home before dark lest "the cloth come looking for company." And when the night wind stirs through the rice fields and a white scrap flutters by, the elders smile faintly and say, "Don't grab it. It may be lonely."

jorōgumo

shapeshifters, tricksters and illusions

silk-spinning enchantress

Within the folds of Japanese mountain mist and beyond the echoes of remote waterfalls, whispers tell of a woman too beautiful to be real. Draped in a silken kimono, with eyes that seem to see into the soul, she offers travelers tea, music, or soft words. Those who follow rarely return. This is the Jorōgumo, the "Binding Bride" or Spider Woman, a yōkai of terrifying duality—half human, half monstrous spider—who spins webs not just from silk, but from seduction, illusion, and fate.

The earliest known mention of the Jorōgumo appears in Edo-period writings, particularly the Konjaku Hyakki Shūi by Toriyama Sekien in the 18th century, though her roots run deeper into regional folklore. Her name literally translates to "prostitute spider" or "entangling bride," and she is often said to be a large orb-weaving spider that, upon reaching 400 years of age, gains the ability to shapeshift into a beautiful woman. From that moment, her hunger turns from insects to humans, favoring young, unsuspecting men who stumble into her lair.

Jorōgumo legends are localized in various regions, with the most famous tales emerging from Jōren Falls in Shizuoka Prefecture. There, it's said she resides beneath the rushing water, emerging to lure travelers and fishermen into her web. Some stories describe her playing a biwa (a traditional lute) to charm passersby; others tell of a sudden tug at the feet as she pulls her victims beneath the surface. Few who hear her song can resist, and fewer still return to speak of it.

What makes the Jorōgumo so chilling is the seamlessness of her deception. She does not attack in a monstrous form outright. Instead, she blends into society, often presenting herself as a vulnerable woman in need of help, a musician in a lonely hut, or a grieving widow. The transformation occurs gradually, and only too late does the unfortunate soul realize that the beautiful hostess is spinning silk with unnatural grace, her fingers growing longer, her robes hiding something monstrous beneath.

Unlike demons of brute strength, Jorōgumo uses manipulation and beauty as her tools. In this way, she reflects a deep cultural fear of illusion—of being unable to distinguish between what is real and what is peril. She is a reminder that even grace can be lethal, and that some dangers do not roar, but whisper sweetly. As with many yōkai, her myth carries undertones of caution: to beware the unknown, to listen to one's instincts, and not to stray too far from the familiar paths of the world.

Throughout literature and ghost stories, the Jorōgumo often plays the role of both predator and punishment. She preys upon vanity, lust, and loneliness, drawing those who seek comfort or admiration into their final embrace. But not all tales end in death. Some stories suggest that if one sees through her illusion and shows no fear, she may simply vanish or even retreat in shame. Her power, after all, is rooted in deception—and once revealed, the spell is broken.

Unlike other yōkai who wander freely, the Jorōgumo is often tied to a specific location, her web anchored to a physical threshold—be it a forest glade, a waterfall, or an abandoned shrine. Her presence marks a place where reality thins, and where beauty and terror coexist in silken silence. She does not rampage or haunt randomly; she waits, watches, and chooses. In this restraint lies her true terror: not in what she does, but in how easily she can appear where you least expect—smiling, waiting, weaving.

kamaitachi

shapeshifters, tricksters and illusions

sickle weasels

Across Japan's snowbound plains and mountain passes, people once feared the bite of invisible blades. A man walking through a sudden gust might feel a sharp sting across his leg — and when he looked down, blood flowed from a cut as clean as a knife's edge. There was no attacker, no sound, only the whirling cry of the wind. From these mysteries came the tale of the Kamaitachi, the "sickle weasels," swift yokai said to ride the rushing gusts and strike before breath could even be drawn.

In the folklore of Nagano, Niigata, and Tohoku, the Kamaitachi are described as three spirits working in unison. The first knocks down the victim with a blast of wind, the second slashes with razor claws, and the third applies a strange salve that prevents death but leaves the wound bloodless and aching. This strange mercy — injury without killing — set them apart from darker yokai. They were tempests given form, mischievous more than murderous, children of the mountain storms who danced in laughter as men cursed the wind.

Some storytellers imagined them as spirits of the itachi, the weasel, small but fierce creatures already linked with supernatural cunning. Others saw them as embodiments of the north wind itself, the sharp edge of winter that cuts through clothes and flesh alike. Their attacks were said to occur suddenly and without warning, especially when the wind twisted into a whirlwind. Villagers would bow to passing gusts or whisper offerings into the air, hoping to appease the unseen hunters within.

During the Edo period, healers and monks debated the nature of Kamaitachi wounds. The cuts were always shallow, clean, and painless until the bleeding began. Physicians called it a cold injury; peasants insisted it was yokai work. In either case, the phenomenon deepened Japan's respect for nature's unseen forces — a belief that even a moment's breeze might conceal intelligence, intention, and spirit. Mountains were not merely landscapes; they were living bodies through which invisible beings moved.

Depictions of the Kamaitachi vary wildly, from furry weasels with scythe-like claws to streaks of silver slicing through the sky. In some regions they were even honored as minor gods of wind and speed, protectors of travelers who carried offerings of sake or rice balls into the mountains. Artists of the Meiji era painted them as half-weasel, half-human figures spinning within tornadoes, eyes gleaming like cold fire. Their claws gleamed with motion itself — symbols of precision, swiftness, and the razor-thin boundary between harm and grace.

In the poetry of Bashō's followers, the Kamaitachi embodied the loneliness of winter travel. "A cut of wind, unseen — it leaves no wound but memory," wrote one wandering monk, turning the yokai into a metaphor for life's sudden pain. Each invisible strike became a reminder of impermanence, a passing moment of beauty and hurt carried on the breath of the world. In this sense, the Kamaitachi was both monster and muse, the swift spirit of transition itself.

Modern Japan still keeps the weasel wind alive. It appears in anime, woodblock revival art, and even local mascots, its once-feared image transformed into a charming symbol of mountain folklore. Yet the chill remains in the tale's heart — that wind can wound without being seen, and that even the smallest creature may carry the strength of the storm. Somewhere between the rush of air and the silence that follows, the Kamaitachi still dances unseen, laughing in the space between one heartbeat and the next.

kasa-obake

shapeshifters, tricksters and illusions
hopping umbrella

When the rain begins to whisper against the tiled roofs and the wind rustles through paper screens, some swear they hear the rhythmic thump... thump... thump of a single wooden leg hopping down the street. A flash of color, a rolling eye, a flickering tongue — and then, nothing but laughter fading into the drizzle. That is the sound of Kasa-obake, the "umbrella ghost," a playful and enduring figure among the tsukumogami, objects that come to life after a hundred years of use or neglect.

The tale begins in the households of old Japan, where possessions were cherished for generations. Lanterns, brushes, sandals, and umbrellas were mended, patched, and passed down until they seemed to carry their own memories. Folklore says that after a century of loyal service, a spirit awakens within them — not to harm, but to remind the living of gratitude. Thus, an abandoned paper umbrella, warped by years of sun and rain, might one night stretch its bamboo ribs, blink open a single enormous eye, and begin to move. Its handle twists into a leg, its ribs form arms, and its laughter echoes softly through the rain.

Unlike the fearsome demons of the mountains or the vengeful spirits of the sea, Kasa-obake is mostly harmless. He startles travelers, peeks through doorways, and spins in circles beneath lantern light. Yet beneath the humor lies something more tender: a spirit born from forgetfulness. The yokai is said to appear when a beloved tool or object is thrown away carelessly, its soul unwilling to fade into oblivion. In his one-legged dance, there is a trace of longing — for purpose, for memory, for recognition.

Old Edo tales describe him as a member of a larger family of tsukumogami — animated possessions awakened during the festival of Obake Yashiki, when spirits were said to roam alongside humans. On those nights, the Kasa-obake would hop alongside other living tools — a sake jug humming drunken songs, a sandal muttering prayers, a lantern grinning with fire in its belly. Together they formed a parade of forgotten things, rejoicing for one night before returning to dust. In this way, the yokai's laughter carried both joy and sorrow — the sound of things once useful remembering what it felt like to be loved.

The image of the umbrella spirit became so iconic that it outgrew its mythic roots. Artists of the Edo and Meiji eras filled picture scrolls and yōkai emaki with his form — one eye wide as the moon, tongue dripping with mirth. Kabuki plays and later kamishibai street theater portrayed him as a comic figure, a trickster who slips between worlds. Yet even in jest, he represented something profound: the spirit of mono no aware, the bittersweet beauty of transience. Every object, like every life, eventually wears thin, but within that fragility lies its soul.

In villages, parents used to warn their children not to mistreat household items. "Handle your umbrella kindly," they said, "or it may grow an eye and come knocking tonight." These words carried both superstition and wisdom — a reminder that respect extends beyond people to the tools and gifts that sustain them. The Kasa-obake thus became a moral teacher wrapped in laughter, showing that even the smallest things deserve reverence.

The hopping umbrella endures as a beloved icon of folklore. It appears in festivals, cartoons, and paintings, his long red tongue wagging in cheerful mischief. Yet his message remains timeless: neglect nothing that has served you well, for gratitude is the thread that binds the living and the inanimate alike.

kitsune

shapeshifters, tricksters and illusions

shifting tails of illusion

Beneath the silver hush of Japanese moonlight, when rice fields shimmer and lanterns tremble in the wind, a fox may cross the path — and that is where the world begins to blur. To see such a fox is to meet a being older than memory, cleverer than men, and infinitely more mysterious. The Kitsune, shapeshifting fox spirit, moves between the sacred and the profane, a bridge between mortal folly and divine cunning. To follow its trail is to lose the boundary between dream and waking, truth and illusion.

In Shinto belief, foxes are sacred messengers of Inari Ōkami, the kami of rice, fertility, and prosperity. Their white forms guard shrines across the countryside, mouths often carved holding keys to granaries or ears of grain. Yet even divine messengers have wild hearts. The same creature that brings blessing can also weave deception. The folk say a Kitsune's power grows with age — every hundred years it gains another tail, until at nine tails it glows with celestial fire and wisdom bordering on divinity. When the ninth tail blooms, even the gods bow to its cunning.

Few yokai embody duality so perfectly. Some Kitsune serve Inari faithfully, guiding the lost, blessing households, and punishing the cruel. These are the zenko, or "good foxes," radiant beings of white and gold. Their counterparts, the yako, are mischievous tricksters who delight in illusion — seducing humans, possessing the greedy, or leading travelers astray beneath the moon. But even the so-called wicked fox is rarely evil; its tricks are mirrors held to human weakness, reflecting our vanity and deceit. A man who chases beauty through the night may wake with straw in his arms, realizing he has courted a fox disguised as a woman.

Tales of fox wives and fox brides thread through the centuries like silk. In one story, a kind farmer saves an injured fox, only to find a mysterious woman waiting at his door the next morning. They marry, live happily, and bear a child — until one day she is seen combing her fur beneath the moonlight. Realizing she has been discovered, she vanishes, leaving only her love behind. The child of such unions, it is said, inherits the Kitsune's eyes: bright, golden, and far too knowing. These stories speak less of trickery than of the bittersweet nature of love itself — fleeting, beautiful, impossible to hold.

The Kitsune's shapeshifting powers are bound to flame and illusion. They can conjure kitsunebi, or foxfire — floating orbs of spectral light that dance across fields and rivers, leading wanderers to danger or revelation. A skilled fox can assume any form, though mirrors and dogs reveal its disguise. In older villages, those suspected of fox possession were feared and revered alike; some saw them as cursed, others as blessed intermediaries who could speak with the unseen. Monks and priests sometimes performed rites to release the trapped fox spirit, chanting to lure it away with offerings of abura-age, the fried tofu said to be a fox's favorite food.

Artists of the Heian and Edo periods found endless fascination in the fox's dual nature. In paintings and kabuki, Kitsune appeared as beautiful women with tails hidden under silks, or as ghostly animals wreathed in flame. Their eyes were always the same — piercing, watchful, and amused by human folly. In literature, they became metaphors for the hidden and the mutable, for desire that both enlightens and destroys. The Japanese heart, so attuned to impermanence, found in the Kitsune a perfect embodiment of beauty's treacherous edge.

mujina

shapeshifters, tricksters and illusions
faceless trickster

Travelers on lonely Edo roads often told of meeting a kind stranger by the roadside — perhaps a weeping woman or a monk carrying a lantern. They would pause to offer help, only for the figure to lift its head and reveal a smooth, blank face: no eyes, no nose, no mouth, only pale skin gleaming under the moon. By the time the scream reached the trees, the stranger was gone, replaced by a plump badger trotting into the brush. Such were the encounters with Mujina, Japan's elusive faceless shapeshifter.

Though often mistaken for Tanuki or Fox spirits, the Mujina is its own breed of mischief. In origin, it was simply a badger — a humble creature of the fields and riverbanks. But folklore transformed it into a master of disguise, a creature whose magic lay not in imitation but in erasure. Where other yokai mimic the faces of others, the Mujina steals faces away, leaving only a blank surface that mirrors the emptiness of the night itself. Its presence chills precisely because it reveals nothing.

Not every tale of the Mujina ends in fear. In some regions, it is seen as playful, teasing passersby to provoke laughter rather than terror. It may leap from the roadside in human form, bow politely, and then reveal its featureless face before bursting into delighted laughter as it disappears. But other stories are darker: travelers led astray into forests, hypnotized by the faceless figure until they wander for days. Priests in the Edo period described these encounters as warnings from the spirit world — reminders that curiosity and fear often share the same root.

Legends collected from the plains of Kyushu and the forests of Chiba describe entire families of Mujina living in burrows near shrines, coming out at dusk to mimic human behavior. They were said to hold small lanterns, imitate laughter, and even join festival processions in disguise. Yet those who followed too closely might glimpse their true form: the tail of a badger slipping beneath the robes, or the faint shimmer of fur beneath the skin. The faceless mask was their strongest illusion, a symbol of how even identity could dissolve into the night.

Writers of the Edo and Meiji periods were captivated by the Mujina's paradoxical charm. Lafcadio Hearn's retelling in the 19th century immortalized the creature in Western imagination: a lone man on a dark road comforts a sobbing woman, only for her to raise her head and show the smooth, blank expanse of her face. His story ends with the man driven mad, muttering "Mujina" in terror, proof that what frightens most is not the monstrous, but the utterly unreadable. The tale spread through Tokyo like wildfire, whispered in alleyways and teahouses whenever the night grew too still.

Artists, too, found fascination in the balance of innocence and horror. Ukiyo-e prints often depicted the yokai with exaggerated roundness — almost cute, yet deeply uncanny. The blank face became a canvas for imagination: it could seem sorrowful, mocking, or completely empty, depending on how the light touched it. Scholars of later centuries compared the Mujina to a living noppera-bō, the faceless human ghost, though older traditions keep them distinct — the former an animal-born trickster, the latter a soul cursed by karma or deceit.

In truth, the Mujina's legend embodies one of Japan's oldest fears: the loss of self. To see a face without features is to glimpse the boundary between form and void, identity and nothingness. Its tales remind listeners that appearances, names, and masks are fragile — easily taken, easily lost.

nure-onna

shapeshifters, tricksters and illusions
dripping serpent

Beneath Japan's rain-drenched skies, when rivers swell and mist clings to the earth, travelers speak of a woman by the water's edge. Her hair is long and dripping, her pale arms cradle what seems to be a newborn child, and her voice trembles with desperate pleading. But when pity leads a passerby closer, the bundle shifts — revealing not a baby, but stones wrapped in wet cloth — and the woman's body uncoils into the glistening length of a serpent. This is Nure-onna, the "Wet Woman," one of Japan's most beautiful and terrifying water spirits.

Her legend drifts from coast to coast, changing with every current. In some provinces she is a river yokai haunting flooded crossings; in others, a sea demon born from drowned mothers and betrayed brides. She appears on stormy nights when the tide rises too fast or the river roars too loud, her form shining with the sheen of rain. The name "Nure-onna" comes from her soaked hair — black as ink and alive with movement — said to glimmer like eel-skin in moonlight. Those who meet her speak of the sound of dripping water that never ends, even when she vanishes.

The most famous version tells of the Izu Peninsula, where fishermen returning from the sea encountered a weeping woman holding a swaddled infant on the rocks. When one man, moved by compassion, offered to hold the baby, it grew impossibly heavy in his arms. As he struggled, the woman's eyes blazed gold, her hair lashed like whips, and her lower body unfurled into a serpent that dragged him screaming beneath the waves. Others say she appeared near rivers during floods, testing human kindness: to those who ignored her, she brought ruin; to those who stopped, she revealed the weight of false compassion.

In the mountains of Kyushu, however, the story softens. There she is seen not as a monster but as a guardian of rivers and children's souls — a once-human woman transformed by grief. Unable to save her child from drowning, she became one with the water, forever seeking to cradle what she lost. Her serpent form embodies both punishment and mourning: a reminder that nature's power to nurture is also the power to destroy. Villagers left offerings of combs and mirrors by riverbanks, believing she lingered to comb her hair in remembrance of what was taken from her.

Artists of the Edo and Meiji periods captured Nure-onna as both alluring and dreadful. In scrolls, her half-human, half-serpent body coils across the page like a living current; her face, though pale and calm, carries an otherworldly sadness. The delicate brushwork of her hair was said to symbolize the fluidity of illusion — beauty, danger, and grief woven into a single stroke. To see her was to see the river's heart: placid at dawn, lethal by dusk.

Her myth reveals Japan's deep reverence for water as both giver and taker of life. The Nure-onna stands where moral and natural forces converge — warning travelers not only to respect the river, but to beware the burden of false mercy. Her dripping hair, eternally wet, symbolizes attachments that cannot be dried or forgotten. Like the water she embodies, she takes the shape of whatever heart she meets: a mother to the lost, a curse to the unkind, a mirror to those who mistake pity for love.

Even in modern Japan, she flows through art and film, her form shifting with each retelling. When the rivers rise and the rain sings against the window, one might feel her presence in the rhythm of the storm: a soft, ceaseless sound, as if someone by the water were still combing her long, wet hair.

obake-inu

shapeshifters, tricksters and illusions

spectral hound of devotion

When travelers speak of soft footsteps behind them on lonely roads, of gentle panting in the dark though no dog is there, they say the spirit of an Obake-inu is passing by. The name simply means "ghost dog," but the stories behind it carry tenderness rather than terror. Unlike vengeful yokai or mischievous tricksters, the Obake-inu is born of loyalty too deep to rest — the spirit of a dog who continues to protect, love, or wander long after its body has returned to the earth.

In many Edo-period villages, dogs were guardians of the threshold, keeping watch at temple gates and family homes. When one died in service — defending a child, warning of fire, or guiding travelers through fog — its spirit was said to rise as an Obake-inu, returning on moonlit nights to complete its duty. Locals left bowls of water or rice outside their doors, whispering thanks to unseen paws that padded softly across their porches. To meet one was considered an omen of safety, as if the boundary between the living and the divine had thinned just enough for devotion to step through.

But not all such spirits were peaceful. Some Obake-inu were born from cruelty: dogs abandoned, beaten, or starved by unkind masters. Their ghosts returned not to harm, but to remind — haunting doorways, appearing in dreams, or howling outside the homes of those who wronged them. Their presence was heavy with sorrow, and yet they rarely attacked. Instead, they lingered until repentance was offered — a bowl of food at a shrine, a prayer spoken aloud, or a single tear shed in remorse. Only then would they fade into the wind, leaving behind the scent of rain and the echo of a wagging tail.

In other tales, the Obake-inu assumes a protective form, guarding travelers through storms or over dangerous bridges. A man might find a stray dog walking beside him in the rain, only to turn and see it vanish when dawn arrives. In these stories, the yokai's silence speaks louder than words: a reminder that love, once given freely, never fully dies. Buddhist monks likened such spirits to bosatsu of the animal realm — beings who linger out of compassion, delaying their next life to shield others from harm.

Art of the Edo and Meiji periods depicted the Obake-inu as both haunting and holy. Scrolls showed translucent hounds curled beside tombs or sitting before temple lanterns, eyes half-closed as if listening to a prayer. Poets wrote of them as "moon dogs" — guardians of memory and loyalty. Their spectral bodies symbolized not vengeance, but continuity: the persistence of kindness in a world prone to forgetting. A carved wooden figurine of a sitting dog, placed near a gate or hearth, was thought to keep its spirit content, preventing it from wandering restlessly.

Regional variations colored the legend further. In the north, some Obake-inu were said to herd spirits of the dead along the riverbanks toward the afterlife, much like the Western psychopomp hounds. In the coastal towns of Shikoku, fishermen told of glowing dogs running across the waves before storms, warning them to stay ashore. In each version, the creature's heart remains constant — unwavering loyalty, even beyond the grave.

Films, manga, and folklore festivals often depict the Obake-inu as a gentle companion to lost souls, or as a symbol of protection for those who wander too far into grief. Its legend reminds listeners that devotion, once born, cannot truly perish. When the night grows quiet and the wind shifts softly, some still place a hand to the ground, feeling the faintest vibration — as though an invisible tail had just brushed by in thanks, before vanishing into the dark.

rokurokubi

shapeshifters, tricksters and illusions

sleepless neck of hidden sin

In the gentle hush of a summer night, when the paper walls breathe and the lamp flickers low, a woman's head may begin to drift. It rises slowly, tethered to her body by an impossibly long, snake-like neck that coils through the dark like a living shadow. The rest of her form remains still beneath her quilt, breathing softly as if dreaming. Those who witness such a sight soon learn they have met a Rokurokubi, one of Japan's most quietly terrifying yokai — a creature whose curse is not malice, but unconfessed longing.

By daylight, she appears entirely human. Her laughter rings clear in the marketplace; she bows politely at temple gates. But when night descends, her spirit slips its leash. Some say her neck stretches because her soul seeks freedom from guilt or desire. Others claim it is punishment — a karmic deformity bestowed upon those who mocked priests, broke vows, or scorned the sacred. Whatever its cause, the result is the same: when sleep comes, the Rokurokubi's head wanders, feeding on the fear or dreams of those nearby, and by dawn returns to rest as if nothing had stirred.

In early Edo folklore, the curse often fell upon women who carried secret burdens — widows, geisha, and wives of traveling merchants. Their yearning, trapped between duty and longing, twisted into supernatural form. While their bodies remained bound by social restraint, their necks reached outward, exploring the forbidden spaces of night. The Rokurokubi thus became a symbol not of evil but of repression: an echo of voices silenced by expectation, a nightmare born from the ache of confinement.

Some stories render her gentle. A woodcutter once offered shelter to a weary woman; waking in the night, he saw her head gliding about the rafters like a drifting lantern. Yet she did not harm him. When dawn broke, she wept and confessed her curse — that each night her head left her body to wander, yearning for the world she could never touch. In gratitude for his silence, she vanished into the forest, leaving only a single strand of hair caught on the beams, long as a river reed. Such tales portray her not as predator, but as tragic wanderer.

Others, darker, tell of Rokurokubi who lost control of their nocturnal hunger. Their floating heads licked the lamp oil from lanterns, whispered madness into sleepers' ears, or drank the lifeforce of passing travelers. The more they fed, the longer their necks grew, until they could no longer return. These became the nukekubi, whose heads detached entirely and flew on their own, biting and shrieking before dawn forced them back to their decaying shells. In this evolution of the legend, horror overtook sorrow — the punishment for indulgence consuming the cursed.

Artists of the Edo and Meiji periods found irresistible fascination in her shape. Woodblock prints captured her neck looping through doorways or curling among clouds like silk ribbon, juxtaposing beauty with absurdity. Painters treated her elongation as visual poetry — the stretch between body and spirit, between what is shown and what is hidden. In these images, fear gave way to melancholy; her long neck was less a weapon than a confession.

For moralists and priests, the Rokurokubi embodied karmic balance. For poets, she symbolized yearning that outlasts the body's limits. And for common folk, she was a reminder whispered across generations: even the most ordinary heart can harbor something strange in the dark. Each night she rises silently, neck swaying like a willow in the wind, her face luminous with impossible sadness.

tanuki

shapeshifters, tricksters and illusions

drumming trickster

In the twilight hours between laughter and dream, when rice wine warms the air and the wind carries the scent of cedar, one might glimpse a round figure dancing by the roadside — hat tilted, belly bouncing, and eyes full of mischief. That is the Tanuki, Japan's raccoon-dog spirit, master of illusion, good humor, and unexpected wisdom. Among yokai, few are loved more dearly, or forgiven more easily.

The Tanuki's roots run deep in Japanese soil, from ancient Jōmon legends to Heian poetry. Farmers once saw their real counterparts darting through the fields at dusk, their cries like human laughter, their eyes gleaming like lanterns. Over centuries, folklore blurred the line between beast and spirit until the Tanuki became a creature of transformation — one who could change its shape, conjure illusions, and drink merrily with monks and travelers alike. To encounter one was to risk both bewilderment and delight.

Transformation is the Tanuki's art. It fashions itself into priests, merchants, teapots, and even entire inns to trick the unsuspecting. Some tales describe weary travelers who rest in fine lodgings, only to wake in a field surrounded by leaves and laughter. Others tell of Tanuki disguised as statues, bowing silently until the viewer bows back — only to burst out laughing before vanishing into the wind. Yet its pranks rarely wound; they teach humility instead. The yokai reminds mortals that life's riches, like illusions, can vanish in an instant.

The Edo period saw the Tanuki become a folk hero of cheerful mischief. Artists painted him with oversized bellies and comically large scrotums — symbols not of vulgarity, but of luck, wealth, and boundless confidence. Peddlers kept small Tanuki charms in their shops to attract fortune, their round eyes and smiling faces promising prosperity through joy rather than toil. Even as he fooled the greedy, he blessed the kind; even as he played with appearances, he celebrated the spirit behind them.

Some stories soften his laughter into melancholy. In the forests of Shikoku, people speak of Tanuki who fell in love with humans, disguising themselves to live briefly among them before returning to the wild. Others tell of old Tanuki watching villages disappear to time and modernity, drumming sadly on their bellies as rice fields gave way to cities. These tales reveal a gentler spirit beneath the humor — one aware of life's fleeting beauty, one that drinks, laughs, and mourns with equal sincerity.

Shrines and statues dedicated to the Tanuki still stand across Japan, often near tea houses, temples, and roadsides. Each figure carries eight traditional symbols of fortune: the straw hat of protection, big eyes for awareness, a round belly for calm, a sake bottle for virtue, a promissory note for trust, a large tail for steadiness, a kind smile for welcome, and yes — exaggerated anatomy for abundance. Together they form a lesson wrapped in laughter: fortune favors those who live fully, laugh loudly, and trust the road beneath their feet.

In the end, the Tanuki is more than a trickster — it is a spirit of joy in disguise, a reminder that the divine may hide in laughter as surely as in prayer. When the moon rises full and golden, villagers still say they can hear the soft drumming of Tanuki bellies echoing through the hills, a rhythm older than sorrow, older even than song. Follow that sound, and you might find the truth the Tanuki has known all along: that illusion, laughter, and kindness are all part of the same great dance beneath the moon.

tesso

shapeshifters, tricksters and illusions

iron-rat monk of vengeance

In the quiet cloisters of ancient Kyoto, where the incense of prayer once hung thick and the chant of monks echoed like waves, envy once gave birth to a plague. From that envy came a creature neither man nor beast — a swarm given voice, a monk's curse woven into fur and fang. He was called Tesso, the Iron Rat, and his story gnaws still at the edges of faith and fear alike.

Centuries ago, in the eighth century, there lived a priest named Raigō, devoted to the emperor and entrusted with prayers for the birth of a royal heir. When his wish was fulfilled, he expected the emperor's promised reward — the construction of a grand temple for his sect. But the court's favor shifted, and the gift was denied. Betrayed, humiliated, and consumed by bitterness, Raigō secluded himself at Mii-dera, fasting until hatred overtook holiness. His prayers, once for life, turned to curses of ruin. When he died, he did not pass into enlightenment — he returned as a storm of rats.

The creature that arose from his grave was unlike any yokai before it. Cloaked in the remnants of monk's robes, its body pulsed with the movement of a thousand vermin. Temples shuddered beneath the squeal of its swarms. The Tesso led its horde against Enryaku-ji, the rival temple on Mount Hiei that had thwarted his ambitions. For nights uncounted, rats poured through the halls, devouring sacred scrolls, chewing the sutras that once carried the Buddha's words, and leaving behind only shredded paper and silence. The smell of incense was replaced by the stench of gnawed parchment and blood.

This act of desecration struck deep into the heart of Buddhist Japan. The Tesso was no mere monster — it was the embodiment of corruption within faith, the rot that begins when devotion gives way to pride. Scholars later described the tale as an allegory for sectarian strife between rival temples; monks whispered it as a warning that even enlightenment could decay if poisoned by envy. To them, Tesso was the mirror of spiritual downfall — the monk who prayed for purity and achieved only pestilence.

Yet beneath the horror, a strange pity clings to the legend. Raigō's transformation into the Iron Rat was not only punishment but revelation: even rage, once sanctified, can become divine in its own terrible way. Some said that after years of haunting, his spirit grew weary of vengeance and sank into the earth beneath Mii-dera, where a shrine still stands to pacify him. Offerings of rice are left there not to honor the beast, but to soothe the sorrow of the man he once was — a plea for peace between gods and the grudges they cannot always forgive.

Artists of the Muromachi and Edo periods depicted Tesso with grotesque majesty — a monk's skull merged with the muzzle of a rat, robes tattered into nests of vermin, eyes burning like lanterns in a famine. Painters found in him a fusion of sacred and profane, the holiness of prayer twisted into pestilence. In these scrolls, the rats swarm not merely as beasts but as the echo of words once spoken in anger — sutras turned into teeth.

Tesso is said to appear when rivalry corrupts piety, when ambition taints duty, when religion forgets compassion. His whisper is the sound of pages tearing in the dark. His breath is the wind that stirs forgotten shrines. And sometimes, on nights when offerings are left untended, one might hear faint scratching beneath the floorboards of the monastery — the restless prayer of a monk who could not die cleanly.

yuki-onna

shapeshifters, tricksters and illusions

snow woman of silent winter

In the hush of winter nights, when the moon hangs like a shard of ice and the snow falls without sound, travelers speak of a woman walking through the storm. She leaves no footprints, her kimono ripples though no wind stirs, and her face — pale as frost — seems carved from the stillness itself. This is Yuki-onna, the "Snow Woman," whose beauty chills as much as it enchants. She is the spirit of winter personified, both savior and executioner, ghost and goddess of the cold.

Her story drifts through Japan like the snow she commands, changing shape with every telling. In some provinces she is a ghostly maiden who appears during blizzards, luring lost travelers with her impossible grace before exhaling a breath so cold it turns their hearts to ice. In others, she is a lonely soul searching for warmth, punishing cruelty but sparing those who show compassion. Each region agrees on her essence: she is a creature of purity and death, born from the breath of the mountain snows.

One of the oldest tales comes from the province of Echigo. A woodcutter and his apprentice were caught in a snowstorm, seeking shelter in a hut. That night, the door opened, and a woman of dazzling whiteness appeared. She exhaled gently over the older man, freezing him instantly, then turned to the youth and whispered, "Tell no one of what you have seen, and you shall live." Years later, the young man married a beautiful stranger with skin cold to the touch. Only when he confessed his encounter did she reveal herself — the Yuki-onna — and vanished into a flurry of snow, leaving him to cradle empty air.

But not all of her legends end in sorrow. Some claim that Yuki-onna marries mortals out of love, bearing children whose breath clouds even in summer. In these tales, she represents the delicate line between worlds — spirit and flesh, winter and spring. Her nature is bound by balance: she kills the cruel traveler but spares the kind-hearted one; she takes life without malice, like frost that falls without intent. To the mountain villages, she was both warning and wonder — a reminder that beauty and danger often wear the same face.

Artists of the Edo period adored her paradox. In scrolls and prints, she glides across white landscapes painted with barely-there ink, her form almost vanishing into the paper — an echo of impermanence. Poets wrote of her touch as "the silence that follows the final snowfall," an image at once terrifying and tender. Her long black hair against white robes became a visual emblem of contrast, of how life itself stands out only when framed by the inevitability of death.

Some saw in her the spirit of the winter wind, others the ghost of a woman abandoned in the cold. In Buddhist interpretation, she is a wandering soul trapped by attachment, unable to reincarnate because she cannot let go of longing. Every breath she takes drains warmth from the world, yet every glance she casts seems to mourn what she destroys. Thus, the Yuki-onna embodies the eternal struggle between desire and detachment — love that freezes the very heart it seeks to hold.

Even now, her legend endures. Films, art, and stories continue to reimagine her: sometimes as predator, sometimes as protector, always as the personification of winter's beauty and its cruelty. In Japan's northern prefectures, parents still warn children not to wander into the snow after dusk, lest a white woman ask them, "Are you cold?" — for to answer yes is to lose the warmth of your breath forever.

yosuzume

shapeshifters, tricksters and illusions

night sparrow

On narrow mountain trails where the darkness hums and the wind carries strange songs, travelers sometimes hear the soft flutter of wings — a sound too near to be natural, too rhythmic to be wind. Then, from the shadows, a small voice begins to chirp, delicate yet persistent, echoing like laughter behind the trees. That is the Yosuzume, the Night Sparrow, a yokai both feared and revered in Japan's remote highlands, said to appear as twilight deepens into true night.

At first glance, there is little to fear in such a creature. The Yosuzume looks like any ordinary sparrow, only paler, with eyes that glimmer faintly in the dark. Yet its presence is never accidental. In some regions, it heralds misfortune — the spirit of travelers lost to the mountains, warning others to turn back. In others, it is a guide, fluttering ahead to lead wanderers safely through the night. The difference lies not in the bird, villagers say, but in the heart of the listener: those who travel with greed or anger hear a curse in its song, while the pure of heart find protection in its flight.

The earliest written record of the Yosuzume appears in Edo-era kaidan scrolls from Kyushu, where mountain woodcutters spoke of "singing sparrows" that circled travelers until dawn. To ignore their song was to invite danger — cliffs collapsing, paths vanishing, or wolves appearing from nowhere. To answer the call, however, was equally perilous, for the birds' chirps could grow louder, closer, surrounding a person until disorientation set in. Some said the Yosuzume was not a bird at all, but the disembodied soul of a dead sparrow, seeking company in its endless flight.

As with many yokai, the Yosuzume walks the edge between warning and wonder. Hunters of Akita claimed the flock's appearance signaled mountain spirits at work — a divine interference rather than a curse. They would bow their heads when hearing its cry, whispering thanks for safe passage. Elsewhere, the superstition reversed: travelers would cover their faces and hurry away, for to meet the Night Sparrow head-on meant that a yamabiko, a mountain echo spirit, was mimicking its call — and one who heard too long might lose their way not in the forest, but within their own thoughts.

In artwork, the Yosuzume rarely takes center stage. Instead, it drifts through the backgrounds of ukiyo-e and ink scrolls, a faint white silhouette against indigo skies, a suggestion of presence more than a creature itself. Artists captured it as sound given form — the rustle between branches, the faint vibration in the stillness of dusk. Its wings, often painted half-transparent, blur the line between natural and supernatural, life and echo. The bird itself, like its voice, seems to exist in the space between perception and imagination.

Poets found in the Yosuzume a muse of loneliness. Its nocturnal song symbolized unspoken memory — the words that hover at the edge of saying, the breath caught between fear and comfort. "The night sparrow sings," wrote one Edo poet, "and my heart flutters with it — unseen, unheard, untethered." In this way, the yokai became less a monster than a mood, a living metaphor for the quiet uncertainty of night travel and the vulnerability of those who walk alone beneath the moon.

To heed the bird is to trust the unseen; to flee is to cling to the known. Its whisper is the voice of the wild reminding humankind that not all roads are meant to be conquered. And so, when night deepens in the mountains and a faint chirp trembles through the dark, it may be wise to bow lightly, whisper thanks, and walk on — for the Yosuzume's song, like the path ahead, belongs to the mystery of the night.

ao-andon

vengeful spirits and yokai of death
blue lantern of fear's final breath

There was a time in Edo Japan when summer nights rang with the soft rustle of silk and the low murmur of ghost stories. Friends would gather in candlelight to play Hyakumonogatari Kaidankai, the "Game of One Hundred Tales." After each tale, a candle was extinguished, until only one remained. It was said that when the last light flickered out, something unearthly appeared — born from the breath of every whispered fear. That something was Ao-andon, the "Blue Lantern Spirit," the embodiment of all stories come alive.

Her name comes from the paper lanterns that cast a ghostly blue glow, colored by indigo pigment or mica dust, their flames trembling in the humid air. When she appeared, witnesses spoke of a woman's form — pale and beautiful, her face lit by the same blue light that once filled the room. Her hair streamed like ink smoke, and her eyes shimmered like sapphire glass. The scent of burning oil filled the air, and those who gazed too long found themselves entranced, unable to tell whether they were awake or still inside a story.

Ao-andon was not born of vengeance or sin, but of imagination itself. She is the spirit of fear distilled — a being called forth when humans create too much mystery for the world to hold. To summon her is to cross the boundary between teller and tale, for every story leaves a residue of belief, and when a hundred are told in reverence or terror, their collective breath becomes alive. The last candle's dying flame, reflecting in a hundred expectant eyes, is said to be her doorway. Through it, she steps into being — not to harm, but to remind humanity of the power it wields when it dreams too deeply.

In some accounts, she appears only briefly: a woman with blue-tinged skin and blackened teeth, smiling as the final candle gutters out, then vanishing into the smoke. In others, she lingers, whispering new tales to those present, tales that had never been told before — stories that wound into the listeners' minds like ivy, until they began to believe them real. Thus, she became not only a yokai of fear but of creation, the haunting muse of every storyteller who risks summoning something true from imagination.

Artists of the Edo period adored her spectral allure. In ukiyo-e woodblocks, she is painted with the grace of a courtesan and the chill of a ghost — long sleeves flowing like ribbons of water, her skin illuminated by indigo lantern light. Her presence is quiet, elegant, and hypnotic. Unlike monstrous yokai that claw or shriek, Ao-andon seduces through stillness. She reminds the living that fear is most powerful when unspoken, when it hangs suspended in silence like smoke above a dying flame.

To the scholars of the Meiji era, she symbolized a new kind of spirit — one born not of nature but of culture. While foxes, serpents, and demons carried the raw weight of the earth's old fears, Ao-andon carried the echo of human invention. She was the ghost of the mind, the manifestation of what happens when people believe their own stories too deeply. In this sense, she is as modern as she is ancient, forever reborn in each retelling — in every novel, film, and whispered tale told by candlelight.

When someone finishes a tale so perfectly that silence follows — that fragile moment when imagination and fear intertwine — it is said Ao-andon watches from the edge of the room, her smile faint and knowing. For as long as humans gather in the dark to trade stories, the Blue Lantern Spirit will always be there, waiting for the final light to dim.

funayūrei

vengeful spirits and yokai of death
drowned spirits

When the sea darkens under a moonless sky and the horizon disappears into fog, fishermen whisper that the dead are stirring. Out of the waves they rise — pale shapes with dripping hair and hollow eyes — calling softly for help, for warmth, for acknowledgment. These are the Funayūrei, the "Boat Ghosts," spirits of those who perished at sea and cannot find rest. To see them is to glimpse the ocean's memory of every life it has swallowed.

The earliest stories of Funayūrei drift from Japan's coastal villages, where the line between sea and spirit world has always been thin. In times of shipwreck or sudden storm, survivors spoke of hearing their lost crewmates calling from the water, their voices soft as the wind yet close as a whisper in the ear. As years passed, those voices took form: phantom sailors standing on the waves, their white burial robes stained with salt, their faces glistening with seawater instead of tears. Some reached out pleadingly; others beckoned wordlessly for the living to join them below.

According to legend, the Funayūrei travel in spectral fleets, appearing as ghostly boats that mirror the living vessel beside them. Sailors would look out over calm waters only to see their own ship reflected — crew and all — sailing silently across the mist. Then, without warning, pale hands rose from the surface, clutching at the hull, dragging it downward into the dark. The drowned wished for company, for justice, for acknowledgment of their suffering. In this way, the ocean became both grave and mirror, swallowing not only bodies but memories.

Many tales tell of their ritual request for a hishaku, a ladle. When a sailor, out of fear or pity, passed one to them, the Funayūrei would use it to pour endless seawater into his boat until it sank. The only way to survive was to offer a ladle with its bottom missing — a gesture that tricked the ghosts without offending them. This delicate balance between reverence and wit, compassion and caution, shaped Japan's seafaring superstitions for centuries. To the wise, the Funayūrei were not demons but emissaries of the sea's justice — reminders of the respect owed to every life taken by the tide.

In some regions, they were believed to arise during Obon, when ancestral spirits return to visit the living. Families of lost sailors placed lanterns on the waves to guide the Funayūrei home, turning terror into mourning, horror into ritual. The blue glow of those lanterns still shimmers across coastal festivals, each flame a fragile truce between the living and the drowned. The ocean, once feared as their prison, became their temple — its waves the chanting of their ceaseless prayer.

Edo-period artists rendered the Funayūrei with exquisite melancholy. In ukiyo-e prints, they appear as pale women whose hair billows like seaweed, eyes fixed on unseen horizons. Their beauty is cold and luminous, reflecting the paradox of their nature: victims and avengers, mourners and monsters. Writers saw in them Japan's enduring truth — that death and nature are never truly separate, and the sea, however cruel, is both destroyer and mother.

For Buddhist storytellers, the Funayūrei embodied the karmic weight of untimely death. Souls drowned without burial or prayer were believed to wander in anguish, transformed into waves and tempests. Priests recited sutras on the shore to calm them, striking bells whose echoes carried across the surf like wind chimes over water.

gashadokuro

vengeful spirits and yokai of death
giant skeleton of the dead

When the wind sighs over forgotten battlefields and the grass grows thick over nameless graves, some say the ground begins to tremble. From the soil rises a mountain of bone, groaning with the weight of unfulfilled hunger. Its skull blocks the moon, its fingers scrape the stars. This is the Gashadokuro, the "Starving Skeleton," a monstrous spirit born from the agony of those who died without burial or remembrance — a ghost of a thousand ghosts fused into one.

The earliest whispers of the Gashadokuro emerged during Japan's age of endless warfare, when famine and disease claimed more lives than swords. It was said that when many died at once — their bodies left to rot in the open, their bones scattered by rain and crows — their spirits would merge, bound by shared resentment. Their hunger and sorrow solidified into an immense skeletal form that wandered the night, seeking to devour the living who still enjoyed the warmth it had been denied. The crunch of its footsteps was the sound of bones grinding against the memory of the earth.

Legends say the Gashadokuro moves silently until it strikes. Travelers walking alone after midnight hear nothing but the hum of insects before a cold shadow falls over them. Then comes a faint rattle — like teeth chattering — as the giant's skull lowers to peer down. It grabs its prey with hands the size of houses and lifts them to its jagged mouth. Some say it drinks the blood of its victims; others that it merely crushes them to add their bones to its own towering frame. Whatever the version, none who are seen by it are said to escape alive.

Yet not all tellings paint the creature as pure malice. Some stories call it a manifestation of grief rather than hatred — a colossal echo of those denied the dignity of remembrance. In the Heian period, priests spoke of the Gashadokuro as a karmic phenomenon, proof that the bonds of suffering could transcend death. Each bone within its body represented a life forgotten by the living, and every step it took was a demand for memory. To see it, they said, was to witness guilt itself walking upon the earth.

Artists of the Edo era immortalized its terrifying grace. In ukiyo-e prints, the Gashadokuro's skull leers through storm clouds, its eye sockets glowing with ghostly fire. It was often depicted reaching into ruined huts or peering through broken temple roofs, symbolizing the fragility of human shelter before the vastness of death. The creature's size was not just physical but moral — a reflection of how small human compassion can become when weighed against the suffering it forgets.

In some tales, exorcists and onmyōji managed to subdue the Gashadokuro by appeasing the restless dead within it. Offerings of water, food, and sutras were said to weaken its hunger, causing the giant to crumble into dust as each spirit found peace. The sound of its collapse was described as a thousand sighs fading into dawn. But as long as wars were fought and graves left unmarked, the stories insisted the giant would rise again — the earth's own reminder that neglect feeds monstrosity.

Modern retellings keep the Gashadokuro alive as a symbol of collective memory. It appears in literature, art, and film not only as a monster but as a conscience — the embodiment of every forgotten name, every abandoned life. When the wind moans over the hills or a tremor shivers the soil, old villagers still murmur prayers to the unknown dead. For somewhere beneath the ground, bones may still be listening. And if the living grow too careless, the great skeleton may yet rise once more, its hollow eyes alight with the hunger of history itself.

ikiryō

vengeful spirits and yokai of death

living ghost of unspoken torment

Among all the phantoms of Japan's long night of spirits, none are so unsettlingly human as the Ikiryō — the "living ghost." Unlike the shades of the dead, the Ikiryō is the spirit of a person still alive, torn loose by emotions too powerful to remain contained. It walks abroad while its body sleeps or burns with resentment, unseen by all but the sensitive and the doomed. In the silence between breath and thought, the living can become their own haunting.

The earliest mention of Ikiryō appears in the Heian-period literature of courtly Japan, where envy and longing brewed like slow poison in the confines of silk-draped chambers. Noblewomen spoke of unseen presences pressing upon their chests, whispering in familiar voices. The most famous tale is that of Lady Rokujō from The Tale of Genji — a woman whose jealousy over her lover's new consort became so consuming that her spirit slipped free of her body, wandering unseen to torment the rival in her sleep. Even as Lady Rokujō sat composed at court, her ghost committed vengeance on her behalf, her body trembling, her soul aflame.

This idea — that emotion itself can fracture the soul — resonated deeply with Heian belief. In an age where dreams, omens, and unseen forces shaped daily life, the Ikiryō was both proof of passion's power and a warning against its excess. It revealed that hatred, grief, or desire could transform the living into ghosts before death. For priests and poets alike, it blurred the distinction between sin and suffering: the curse of one's own heart turned outward into the world.

Not all Ikiryō, however, were born of malice. Some left their bodies unintentionally, drawn by longing or love. There are stories of travelers who, falling gravely ill far from home, sent their spirits ahead to bid farewell to family. Wives appeared at doorways just as they died in distant lands; mothers were seen sitting beside their children in dreams, their bodies still alive but fading. These gentle manifestations carried no wrath, only sorrow — the soul's yearning to be present where the body could not.

In Buddhist interpretation, the Ikiryō represented attachment at its most dangerous form — the refusal to let go. It was said that when the heart clings too fiercely to a person or grievance, the kon (vital spirit) may split, wandering as a shadow-self. Exorcists were called to perform rites of pacification, not to banish an evil spirit, but to heal the suffering within the living host. The ceremony was both confession and cure, urging the afflicted to release their hatred before it consumed both self and victim.

Artists and playwrights of later centuries transformed the Ikiryō into an emblem of beauty bound to despair. In Noh theater, she appears veiled, her movements slow and dreamlike, her voice drifting between gentleness and fury. The audience watches as her ghostly form dances before the body that birthed her, a performance of emotion uncontained. The mask of the Ikiryō — neither fully human nor monstrous — captures that liminal truth: that the deepest hauntings are not from outside, but from within.

Psychologists and storytellers alike find in the Ikiryō a timeless metaphor — for obsession, for trauma, for the pieces of ourselves we lose to unspoken pain. She is the ghost that lives in every heart that has ever loved too fiercely or hated too long. When a thought will not rest, when a grudge burns cold but refuses to die, that is when the Ikiryō stirs — walking silently through the corridors of the mind, her thread of light still tethered to the living flesh that dreams of her.

iso-onna

vengeful spirits and yokai of death
siren of the rocky shore

When the sea breathes its cold mist over Japan's lonely coasts and the sound of waves becomes almost human, sailors tell of a woman standing upon the rocks. Her figure is pale against the dark horizon, her hair wet and glistening, her gaze unreadable. Those who call to her never return. She is the Iso-onna, the "Woman of the Shore," a sea yokai whose beauty conceals the hunger of the deep.

The legend flows strongest through Kyushu and western Japan, where the boundary between sea and spirit world has always felt perilously thin. In some villages she is a drowned courtesan, cursed to haunt the shore where she met betrayal. In others she is an ancient sea spirit who takes the form of a woman to lure men from their boats. Whatever her origin, the Iso-onna's song is the same — a whisper carried over the water, promising warmth where none exists. To hear it is to feel the pull of the tide inside one's own chest.

Many who vanish at sea are said to have followed her voice. Fishermen tell of glimpsing a woman combing her hair among the rocks, her back turned, her skin gleaming like polished shell. If approached, she lifts her face — and her eyes are hollow, black as the ocean's depth. Some say she smiles before she strikes, dragging her victim beneath the waves with inhuman strength. Others insist she kisses her prey gently before drowning them, her touch as cold as seawater. The only mercy she shows is silence; the sea keeps her secrets well.

Scholars of the Edo period saw in her tale echoes of older water deities — remnants of the Mizu no Kami, the water gods who governed rivers and tides before being forgotten. As faith shifted toward human-centered religions, such spirits were abandoned, their temples left to decay. The Iso-onna may have been born from divine neglect, a goddess turned ghost by the erosion of belief. Her beauty, then, is not vanity but memory: she wears her former divinity like a reflection in dark water, lovely but unreachable.

Yet not all encounters with her end in death. In some coastal folktales, a grieving sailor who lost his wife at sea encounters the Iso-onna during a storm. Instead of taking him, she speaks in his beloved's voice, telling him to return home and care for their child. When he does, he finds the storm has spared his village. The sea, it seems, can be both cruel and kind — and the Iso-onna, like the tide itself, decides which face to show. These stories reveal her dual nature: not a mere monster, but the embodiment of the sea's living will.

Artists often captured her as a figure of haunting grace. In Edo prints, she rises from crashing surf, half-draped in translucent robes, hair whipping like seaweed in the wind. Painters highlighted her white skin against the deep indigo of the waves, portraying her not as a demon but as the soul of the ocean itself — alluring, merciless, eternal. To the Japanese imagination, her image merged the sensual and the sacred, the feminine and the abyss.

Fishermen avoid calling out at night on the open sea, for to answer a strange voice in the wind invites her attention. And when the tide turns strange and the moonlight glows too brightly upon the rocks, villagers close their shutters and whisper old prayers, knowing that beauty seen upon the sea at midnight is never meant for mortal eyes.

jibakurei

vengeful spirits and yokai of death

earthbound ghost

In the stillness of abandoned temples, on fields where no birds sing, and in houses where laughter once lived, Japan speaks of a spirit that never moved on. It is called the Jibakurei, the "Earthbound Ghost." Unlike other yokai that wander or return by will, the Jibakurei is trapped — its essence fused to the very soil where it met its end. To encounter one is to step into the wound of time itself, still open, still bleeding memory into the air.

The origins of Jibakurei reach deep into Japan's spiritual belief in tsukumogami and onryō, spirits that linger out of attachment or rage. But where an onryō seeks revenge and a tsukumogami awakens through use, a Jibakurei remains because it cannot go. Its soul is imprisoned by the gravity of its own death. Whether through violence, sorrow, or unfinished vows, something in the final breath binds it to the earth — and the earth, in return, will not let go.

Many Jibakurei are said to haunt the sites of disaster: burned temples, execution grounds, and forgotten battlefields. In times of war, villagers told of hearing faint weeping where soldiers fell, or of shadows standing guard in ruined watchtowers long after the armies had gone. Some believed the spirits chose to remain — loyal even in death, their duty unfulfilled. Others whispered that the land itself had devoured their souls, feeding on blood until memory became form. To cross such ground was to feel the heaviness of unseen eyes and the weight of lives unacknowledged.

In mountain shrines and village crossroads, gentle Jibakurei linger as guardians, watching over the places they loved in life. A mother's spirit might remain by her child's home; a monk's soul might guard the site of his hermitage. These benevolent forms radiate calm rather than terror, though even they cannot leave their sacred boundary. To pray to them is to offer both compassion and release, acknowledging the sorrow that keeps them tethered like lanterns too dim to rise.

The belief in Jibakurei shaped many of Japan's purification rituals. When new homes or buildings were raised, priests performed jichinsai — ground-pacifying ceremonies — to honor any spirits still tied to the site. Offerings of sake, salt, and rice were buried in the foundations, meant to soothe what could not depart. If strange accidents or cold drafts followed despite the rite, people said the Jibakurei had not yet accepted its peace, and further prayers were required to coax its heart into silence.

Artists and storytellers found deep fascination in the Jibakurei's stillness. In ukiyo-e paintings, these spirits appear half-merged with landscape — their faces fading into clouds, their limbs dissolving into soil. Unlike the violent energy of other ghosts, they emanate a heavy quiet, as if their very being has become the memory of place. Writers of the Edo period often used them as symbols of guilt and remembrance, the echoes of a nation that could not escape its own past.

In modern Japan, the idea of Jibakurei endures in both folklore and pop culture, its image shifting from ancient myth to urban legend. Sites of accidents, suicides, or natural disasters are often spoken of as "cursed grounds" haunted by spirits who died there, unable to move on. Yet beneath the superstition lies an enduring empathy — the recognition that even pain seeks acknowledgment. A Jibakurei does not wander to harm, but to be remembered. To light incense in such a place, to bow one's head even briefly, is to whisper to the unseen: You were here. You still are.

kuchisake-onna

vengeful spirits and yokai of death
slit-mouthed woman

It begins with a question whispered through Japan's foggy streets: "Am I beautiful?"

Those who hear it glance up to find a woman standing just beyond the pool of lamplight — elegant, silent, face half-hidden behind a white mask. She waits for the answer, her eyes gleaming through strands of black hair. If the reply is yes, she reaches up and pulls the mask aside, revealing a mouth sliced from ear to ear. "Even now?" she asks. By the time the second answer comes, it is already too late. This is the Kuchisake-onna, the Slit-Mouthed Woman — a modern nightmare born from ancient fears.

The roots of her legend stretch deeper than the neon streets she now haunts. In older tales, she was said to be a samurai's wife, renowned for her beauty and vanity. When her infidelity was discovered, her husband slashed her face from ear to ear, crying, "Who will think you beautiful now?" Betrayed and broken, she died of her wounds — but her fury outlived her flesh. Her spirit rose, masking her deformity behind cloth or paper, forever seeking reassurance she can no longer believe. What began as personal tragedy became a haunting that mirrors society's obsession with appearances.

Her story resurfaced centuries later in the 1970s, during Japan's urban anxieties and the rise of masked commuters. Reports spread of a mysterious woman approaching children on their way home from school, asking her fatal question. Police received dozens of calls; parents refused to let children walk alone. Newspapers hinted at panic, but folklore scholars recognized the pattern: a timeless yokai reborn in modern form. The Kuchisake-onna was no longer a ghost of feudal jealousy — she was the spirit of collective unease, the face of a culture masked by fear and conformity.

She is said to carry large scissors or a blade, her movements eerily calm. Some stories claim that those who answer "no" are slain instantly; those who say "yes" are rewarded with the same smile she bears. Clever folklore offers ways to escape her — by answering ambiguously ("You are average"), throwing candy to distract her, or asking her the same question in return, confusing her reflection of desire. Yet every version returns to the same tension: beauty and horror, truth and deception, love and mutilation — all bound by the same fragile mask.

Psychologically, the Kuchisake-onna embodies Japan's duality between restraint and repression. Her mask reflects a culture of politeness and concealment; her wound, the violence that festers beneath it. In her smile, the polite façade of daily life splits apart to reveal the pain of being judged, rejected, or forgotten. Like many yokai, she is less monster than mirror — her knife not a weapon, but a metaphor for the self-inflicted wounds of vanity and shame. Beneath her cruelty lies the echo of every voice that ever whispered, "Am I enough?"

Artists have reimagined her endlessly — in ukiyo-e inspired ink paintings, horror films, manga, and digital art. Some render her face sorrowful rather than monstrous, the mask slipping not in rage but in grief. Others cast her as a wandering avenger of abused women, punishing those who exploit beauty and power. Her dual nature — victim and predator, horror and heartbreak — allows her to evolve with each generation, adapting to new fears as effortlessly as she once slipped through Kyoto's mist.

nopperabō

vengeful spirits and yokai of death

faceless ghost of vanished identity

The night in Japan has always been filled with whispers, but none quieter — or colder — than those surrounding the Nopperabō, the Faceless Ghost. It takes the shape of an ordinary human: a merchant, a monk, a lover, even a friend. Everything seems familiar — the voice, the manner, the movement — until, without warning, the face melts away, leaving a blank expanse of smooth skin. No eyes to meet, no mouth to speak, no expression to hold. The horror lies not in what it does, but in what it takes away — the comfort of recognition.

Unlike the vengeful onryō or the monstrous yokai of the mountains, the Nopperabō belongs to the urban shadows of Edo and Meiji Japan, haunting roads, bridges, and riverbanks. It was said to appear at twilight, when the human mind is most uncertain of what it sees. Travelers returning home late would meet a stranger who politely greeted them, perhaps even asked for directions. Then, with a single gesture — a hand across the face — the features vanished. The victim fled screaming, only to find that even those they met afterward wore the same faceless mask.

The most famous tale tells of Akasaka's Nopperabō, recorded by Lafcadio Hearn. A weary fisherman, ignoring his wife's warnings, took the road to Edo at night. At the bridge, he met a young woman weeping. When he approached to comfort her, she raised her face — and revealed nothing. Terrified, he ran home, only to find his wife waiting with concern. As he gasped out the story, she murmured, "Like this?" and rubbed her own face blank. The fisherman's scream was said to echo down the road until dawn.

Interpretations of the Nopperabō are as fluid as the faces it lacks. Some believe it to be a form of mujina, the shapeshifting badger spirit known for illusion and mischief, taking faceless form to frighten humans. Others view it as a kannushi's curse — the lingering energy of forgotten deities erased from memory, wandering the modern world unseen and unacknowledged. To scholars of folklore, the Nopperabō reflects anxiety over the loss of individuality in Japan's rapidly urbanizing society — a spirit born from crowds where everyone began to look the same.

In contrast to its eerie power, the Nopperabō rarely causes physical harm. Its terror lies in revelation: it forces those who see it to confront the void where humanity should be. Edo poets described the encounter as the moment when the familiar ceases to know you. It strips away not just the face, but identity itself — a reminder that form without spirit is nothing more than a shell. The true fear it invokes is not death, but emptiness.

Artists of the Edo period found in the Nopperabō a striking symbol for the fragility of the self. In ukiyo-e prints, the yokai's featureless faces gleam softly under the moon, human in posture yet utterly alien. Their blankness reflects the beauty of restraint — the terror of silence in a culture that prizes form and etiquette. Painters often left their features incomplete on purpose, leaving the viewer to fill in what was missing — only to realize there was nothing to fill.

In the modern age, the Nopperabō endures as a symbol of anonymity — the ghost of a world where faces hide behind masks, screens, and formal smiles. Its blank visage mirrors the subtle horror of losing one's individuality amid the crowd. Some say that when walking home late at night,

oiwa

vengeful spirits and yokai of death
lantern ghost of poisoned beauty

Among all of Japan's onryō — spirits of wrathful women betrayed in life — none burns brighter in legend than Oiwa, the ghost of Yotsuya Kaidan, the Tale of Yotsuya. Hers is not the story of a monster, but of a woman whose suffering transcended death, her sorrow transforming into eternal power. She is the specter who taught Japan to fear injustice — and to respect the pain it leaves behind.

Her story begins in Edo, in the early 19th century, when the samurai Iemon Tamiya, fallen from grace, sought to restore his fortune through deceit. He was married to Oiwa, a devoted woman of quiet beauty and steadfast heart. Yet when Iemon's ambition drew him toward a wealthy bride, he conspired to rid himself of his wife. Through the help of a greedy neighbor, he gave Oiwa poisoned medicine under the guise of a remedy. The venom disfigured her face, twisting one eye downward and rotting her flesh while she still lived. When she saw her reflection in the mirror, horror and heartbreak consumed her — and the pain became her final prayer.

That prayer was heard. Oiwa died, but her spirit refused to rest. Soon after her death, those who betrayed her began to meet grisly fates. Iemon's new bride fell dead on her wedding night, her face taking on Oiwa's twisted features. The conspirators went mad, driven by visions of her distorted countenance peering from lanterns, mirrors, and water bowls. Wherever guilt festered, her spirit appeared — sometimes silent, sometimes whispering her husband's name in a voice colder than the grave.

In kabuki theater, her tale was immortalized by Tsuruya Nanboku IV in Yotsuya Kaidan (1825), where Oiwa's spectral form rises through paper walls, her hair streaming like riverweed, her face half in shadow. The audience, far from recoiling, was entranced. She was not merely terrifying — she was beautiful in her suffering, a symbol of betrayal that transcended her mortal life. Her story became a mirror of Edo's social conscience, a cry for those silenced by cruelty and injustice. To see Oiwa was to confront the hidden rot behind propriety and power.

Over time, her legend grew sacred. Actors performing Yotsuya Kaidan began visiting her shrine at Myōkō-ji Temple in Tokyo before every production, offering prayers to appease her spirit and avoid misfortune. To neglect the ritual was to court disaster — sets collapsing, actors injured, inexplicable fires consuming stages. Even in modern cinema, directors and crews continue the tradition. Oiwa has become not just a ghost, but a guardian of truth in art: a presence reminding creators that stories of suffering must be told with respect.

Artists rendered her face as both grotesque and divine — one side ravaged by poison, the other still shining with her former beauty. The duality became her signature: love and rage, victimhood and transcendence. Her image appears in ukiyo-e prints, ghost scrolls, and films — each depiction a delicate balance of horror and sorrow. Where other yokai embody the monstrous, Oiwa embodies consequence: she is what happens when compassion is betrayed.

For Oiwa does not simply haunt — she endures, a spirit born from the world's cruelty, teaching that even broken faces can stare back with unflinching truth.

onryō

vengeful spirits and yokai of death
vengeful spirit of unending sorrow

In the dim corridors of Japan's ghostly imagination, few figures loom larger than the Onryō, the "Vengeful Spirit." Unlike wandering souls who seek peace or protection, the Onryō exists to redress wrongs — and her justice is merciless. She rises not from evil, but from injury: a wound so deep that even death cannot contain it. Her wrath is not born of cruelty, but of love betrayed, loyalty broken, and suffering left unanswered. And in her haunting, she becomes eternal.

The origins of the Onryō reach back to the Nara and Heian periods, when Japan's courts trembled at the thought of restless spirits. In those times, people believed that human emotion — on — could corrupt the spirit after death, transforming it into a destructive force. When a person died angry or aggrieved, their soul refused to ascend, instead turning against the living with fire, famine, or plague. Such spirits were not myths but political realities: emperors performed elaborate purification rites to appease them, fearing that misfortune in the land meant an Onryō had been wronged.

The most famous among these ancient tales is that of Sugawara no Michizane, a scholar and statesman exiled unjustly. After his death, lightning struck the imperial palace, killing his enemies one by one. The emperor repented and deified him as Tenjin, the god of scholarship, transforming the Onryō's vengeance into divine protection. Through this act, Japan learned that even rage could become holiness — that in the balance between fury and forgiveness, gods themselves could be born.

But it is in the feminine form that the Onryō found her most enduring face. In kabuki and kaidan stories of the Edo period, she took shape as the betrayed wife, the murdered lover, the servant unjustly slain. Her white burial kimono, her long black hair unbound, and her pale, floating form became the universal language of Japanese horror. Through her, society confronted the hidden violence of its own patriarchy: the woman silenced in life, roaring in death. Characters like Oiwa of Yotsuya Kaidan and Okiku of Banchō Sarayashiki are not simply ghosts — they are moral reckonings.

The Onryō's power is not bound by place or time. She does not haunt the guilty alone; she curses the world itself, warping nature, bringing storms, madness, and decay. Her vengeance is contagious — a spiritual contagion that spreads wherever her story is told. Yet within her terror lies profound sorrow. She punishes not only her betrayers but herself, unable to release the chains of emotion that bind her. In this tragic cycle, she is both executioner and prisoner, a reflection of how love twisted by cruelty becomes destruction.

Artists and playwrights have long reveled in her paradox. In ukiyo-e prints, she floats weightless, one sleeve trailing like smoke, her expression neither wrathful nor serene but heartbreak made visible. Her presence was not painted in blood but in emptiness — a void where humanity once was. She is the ultimate cautionary figure: proof that suffering denied will always find a voice, and that silence, when pressed too long, turns divine.

Each incarnation in modern mythology of Onryō speaks to a new generation's guilt and repression, but her essence remains unchanged: she is emotion without end, grief without grave. The Onryō reminds us that every unburied sorrow will one day rise, that cruelty reverberates beyond the flesh, and that no injustice truly dies — it only waits, patient and pale, for the silence to break.

oni

vengeful spirits and yokai of death
horned demons of storm

From the thunderheads above Japan's mountains to the darkest corners of its folklore, the Oni stride as giants of chaos and fear. With horns jutting from their foreheads, teeth like daggers, and laughter that shakes the earth, they are the monstrous embodiments of punishment — and the wild strength that lies within every human heart. To see one is to stand before the oldest mirror of Japan's soul: both terrifying and profoundly human.

The word oni once meant "hidden," referring not to monsters but to unseen spirits — forces of calamity that brought plague, drought, or madness. Over centuries, these invisible terrors took form, shaped by Buddhist and Shinto thought into horned demons of fury and consequence. They became the jailers of hell, tormenting the wicked, but also the executioners of karmic justice. In this sense, the Oni are not evil for evil's sake; they are the shadows cast by divine order, the punishment that follows when the moral world is broken.

Myth tells that Oni dwell deep in mountains or the caverns of Jigoku, Japan's underworld, where they crush sinners and forge souls anew in fire. Yet many legends place them closer than that — in storm clouds, volcanic peaks, and haunted forests, where they appear as red or blue giants carrying kanabō, their iron clubs. These weapons are not only tools of destruction but emblems of their duty: to break illusion, pride, and deceit. They are fear's artisans, sculpting humility from human arrogance.

Some Oni, however, were once human. Stories tell of monks or warriors whose hatred or greed transformed them into demons after death, their emotions too powerful to dissolve. The legend of Shuten Dōji, the great Oni of Mount Ōe, tells of a once-noble youth whose thirst for rebellion and pleasure turned monstrous. Feasting on travelers and defying the gods, he was finally slain by the hero Minamoto no Raikō — but even dying, he laughed, declaring that righteousness and sin were merely two sides of the same sake cup. In him, Japan saw not just evil, but defiance — the tragic grandeur of the fallen.

Despite their terror, Oni are woven into the rhythms of purification and renewal. During the festival of Setsubun, people cast roasted soybeans while chanting, "Oni wa soto! Fuku wa uchi!" — "Demons out! Fortune in!" Yet even as they banish Oni, they honor them as necessary opposites of the good they invoke. Without darkness, there is no light; without wrath, no mercy. Thus the Oni remain central to Japan's moral cosmology — both destroyers and guardians of order.

Artists of every age have painted them in riotous color: red and blue skins glowing like molten stone, tusks and horns rendered in bold ink. In ukiyo-e prints, they rampage across temples and mountain passes, their power both grotesque and magnetic. Poets likened their roars to thunder and their tears to rain — for even Oni weep, legends say, when the loneliness of eternity overtakes their fury. To depict them is to confront one's own shadow, the part of the self too wild to civilize.

In modern times, the Oni have evolved from pure demons into archetypes of raw emotion. They appear in manga, games, and festivals not merely as monsters but as symbols of endurance and transformation. The red Oni stands for passion, the blue for sorrow; together, they reflect the balance of fire and calm within every heart. Children still wear paper Oni masks at Setsubun, laughing as they chase away evil with beans — a playful echo of an ancient ritual that once trembled with fear.

otoroshi

vengeful spirits and yokai of death

shrine's shaggy sentinel

High above Japan's torii gates, where the lantern light fades and the crows no longer perch, there dwells a creature of patience and judgment. It is the Otoroshi, the "Hairy Guardian," a yokai that waits in silence on temple roofs and sacred thresholds, unseen by the hasty and unmindful. Its body is heavy with matted hair, its claws curved like sickles, and its eyes gleam with the faint red of banked embers. It does not wander. It watches.

Unlike most spirits, the Otoroshi is no trickster nor devourer. It is a warden — a creature tasked with guarding holy ground from the unworthy. In the earliest Edo scrolls, it was said to dwell upon torii, Shinto's symbolic gateways between the mortal and the divine. Travelers passing beneath who showed reverence were blessed by safe passage, but those who entered defiled, laughing, or arrogant were struck down by unseen force. Some stories claim the Otoroshi drops upon them from above like a collapsing shadow, crushing them beneath its weight before vanishing into silence once more.

Its name, "Otoroshi," comes from osoroshii, meaning fearsome or awe-inspiring, though its presence is not always meant to terrify. It embodies the spiritual weight of sanctity — the feeling that certain spaces demand humility. To pass under a shrine gate is to cross a threshold; the Otoroshi ensures that crossing is earned. Thus, even when unseen, it shapes the way people move through sacred places: heads bowed, hearts quieted. It is fear as a form of respect.

Legends vary as to its origin. Some priests claim it was once a divine beast, assigned by the gods to guard their gates for eternity. Others whisper it is the spirit of a slain warrior whose devotion bound him to his shrine. A few even suggest it is not one creature at all but an accumulation of forgotten offerings — incense, hair, blood, prayer — fused by centuries into a living presence. However it came to be, the Otoroshi is less a being than a boundary, its body woven from devotion and decay alike.

Artists of the Edo and Meiji periods portrayed the Otoroshi as both terrifying and strangely peaceful. In ukiyo-e prints, its hair cascades like a waterfall, hiding its massive form while leaving only the burning eyes visible. The torii beneath it often gleams in soft ink tones, emphasizing the contrast between divine stillness and lurking power. It was said that one could sense an Otoroshi's presence when the wind shifted suddenly at a shrine gate, or when birds fell silent as one crossed under the red beams.

Despite its fearsome visage, the Otoroshi's heart is not cruel. It guards temples not out of malice but duty. Some tales even describe it as a lonely being, forgotten by priests who no longer believe, still keeping its watch out of habit and honor. At night, when shrines stand deserted, it hums deep within its chest — a sound between a growl and a chant — echoing the prayers once spoken there. In this way, it embodies the persistence of faith long after the faithful have gone.

Modern depictions reimagine the Otoroshi as both guardian and ghost of devotion itself. In manga and film, it crouches atop skyscrapers and torii alike, watching over cities that have forgotten the gods. Its hair, once temple-black, now ripples with soot and neon, yet its gaze remains the same: steady, ancient, unblinking. The Otoroshi asks no worship — only remembrance. To feel its eyes upon you at a shrine is not to be cursed, but to be reminded that the sacred is never entirely gone, merely waiting for those who still know to look up.

shirime

vengeful spirits and yokai of death

prankster spirit

In the long, haunted night of Japanese folklore, where vengeful ghosts, weeping women, and temple demons prowl, one creature dares to be ridiculous. The Shirime, whose name literally means "butt-eye," turns terror into parody. He walks the moonlit roads of Kyoto, unclothed and unashamed, approaching travelers with eerie politeness — until he bows deeply, lifts his robe, and reveals a single gleaming eye shining where no eye should ever be. Shocked speechless, the witness flees. The Shirime chuckles, and disappears into the mist.

This peculiar yokai first appeared in the Edo-period scrolls attributed to the great storyteller Yosa Buson, who, centuries before becoming one of Japan's most revered haiku poets, also painted whimsical monsters. The Shirime was one of his strangest inventions: not a killer, not a ghost of vengeance, but a walking punchline that mocked fear itself. In a culture where modesty and decorum reigned, the Shirime's very form was a challenge — an irreverent wink, quite literally from behind.

Though its origins seem comedic, deeper meaning clings to its absurdity. Some folklorists see the Shirime as an ancestor of the obscene kami found in ancient fertility rites — remnants of pre-Shinto worship where the body itself was sacred, and humor could ward off evil. In this view, the yokai's luminous eye is not mere mockery, but a purifying force, banishing darkness with laughter. Others interpret it as social satire: a spirit that exposes the human fear of humiliation more than the supernatural itself.

Stories of encounters with the Shirime are rare but vivid. A Kyoto samurai walking home at dusk was once said to have met a stranger who called out politely, "Excuse me, sir." When he turned, the man threw open his robe to reveal the glowing eye and burst into ghostly laughter. The samurai drew his sword — but the figure vanished, leaving only a faint odor of rain and mirth. Ever since, people walking alone near riverbanks or bamboo groves have been warned not to answer voices too politely after nightfall. Courtesy, in Japan, is a virtue — but even politeness has its dangers.

Artists adored the Shirime's audacity. In emaki scrolls, it appears not as grotesque but cheerful, its glowing eye rendered with delicate strokes of gold and silver ink. Edo painters enjoyed the contradiction: a spirit both vulgar and divine, laughter wrapped around a moral. To laugh at the Shirime was to laugh at one's own fear of embarrassment, to accept that even the most refined world hides the ridiculous within.

In modern culture, the Shirime has been resurrected as a figure of surreal comedy — appearing in manga, films, and internet art as both ghost and jester. Some interpret it as an early example of kusogaki energy — the impish chaos that disrupts order and exposes the absurdities of social restraint. It embodies what Japan calls okashii — something strange, funny, and unsettling at once. In a society bound by etiquette, the Shirime offers liberation through laughter, proving that horror and humor share the same trembling heartbeat.

shinigami

vengeful spirits and yokai of death

silent servants of death

In the hush between one breath and the next, when the world stills and time softens, a presence may arrive that is felt more than seen. The Shinigami, or "death gods" of Japanese folklore, are not grotesque beings or cackling reapers, but calm, inevitable figures that guide the dying across the threshold of life. Their name, written with the kanji for "death" (shi) and "god" or "spirit" (kami), reveals their essential role—not as killers, but as escorts for the soul. They are the unseen hand that turns the page, the final companion on the mortal path.

The concept of the Shinigami did not exist in early Japanese religious tradition. Unlike the grim reapers of Western lore, early Shinto and Buddhist belief systems emphasized natural death cycles, karma, and the presence of ancestor spirits rather than personified agents of death. The figure of the Shinigami began to emerge in literature and folklore during the Edo period (1603–1868), influenced in part by imported ideas from Chinese Taoist beliefs and the Western personification of death, introduced during Japan's increasing contact with European culture.

Shinigami appear in various forms across Japanese tales. In some stories, they resemble humans in dark ceremonial robes—silent and pale, faces hidden or hollow-eyed, sometimes carrying lanterns or scrolls bearing the names of the soon-to-die. They may whisper into the ears of those near death or stand at the foot of a bed until the final breath is drawn. Unlike yokai such as the Oni or Nure-onna, Shinigami do not harm. Their presence marks the end, not the cause. They are metaphysical—more essence than entity.

Certain folktales portray Shinigami as deceivers, spirits that tempt humans toward death. One Edo-period story tells of a man who sees a Shinigami beside the bed of a dying person and learns he can steal life by switching the Shinigami's position. But his greed catches up with him, and in the end, death cannot be outwitted. These cautionary tales illustrate how death is not to be manipulated, and those who try to defy its order are punished not by violence, but by inevitability. The Shinigami restores the balance, not through wrath, but certainty.

The Shinigami also reflect deep-rooted fears in Japanese society surrounding lonely deaths, unfulfilled karma, and spiritual unrest. In the early 20th century, especially during times of war and epidemic, their symbolism sharpened. They became emotional representations of despair, suicide, and fate—particularly in rakugo theater and popular ghost stories. In these depictions, they are not evil, but their stillness is disturbing. To see a Shinigami is to be reminded that your thread has been measured, and that what follows is no longer yours to resist.

Shinigami embody the inevitability of all things. They teach that death is not chaos, but structure; not horror, but transition. In Japan's spiritual imagination, where spirits, ghosts, and deities intermingle, Shinigami are not banished—they are accepted. To walk with a Shinigami is not to fight fate, but to recognize it. And in their silent footsteps, many find peace—even if only at the very end.

ubume

vengeful spirits and yokai of death
weeping mother

On nights heavy with rain, when thunder mutters like distant weeping, travelers in Japan's countryside tell of a woman standing by the roadside, cradling a baby in her arms. Her face is pale, her kimono soaked, and her voice trembles with desperation as she pleads for help. Those who take the child from her soon feel it grow heavier and heavier until it becomes a stone or vanishes into mist. By then, the woman is gone — her cries fading into the rain. She is the Ubume, the ghost of a mother who died giving birth, condemned to wander between worlds, forever bound by love that even death cannot quiet.

The earliest records of the Ubume appear in the Konjaku Monogatari-shū (12th century), where she is described as a woman who returns to the world of the living to care for her child. Unlike wrathful spirits, her power is rooted in compassion and sorrow. She is an onryō of love — a mother's final act carried into eternity. The belief stems from Buddhist and folk notions that women who die in childbirth suffer polluted death, denied a peaceful afterlife until their maternal duty is fulfilled. The Ubume's haunting, therefore, is not punishment, but devotion made ghostly.

She appears most often near rivers, bridges, or crossroads — liminal places where life and death blur. Her pale form is said to smell faintly of milk and rain, her steps leaving no trace upon the earth. When she appears to strangers, she offers her child to them with trembling hands. Those pure of heart who hold the infant and survive the encounter are believed to gain blessings — fertility, protection, or safe childbirth — for the Ubume's gratitude softens even her sorrow. But those who refuse or mock her are said to feel her wail echo inside their chest for years, their luck and health withering like flowers without water.

Over time, her image merged with that of Ubumetori, the "birthing bird" spirit — a supernatural being said to lay eggs that hatch into babies, bridging the symbolism of motherhood, creation, and sacrifice. Buddhist priests saw in her the restless compassion of Jizō Bosatsu, the protector of children and travelers; thus, small Jizō statues were erected near riverbanks to console the Ubume and guide the souls of lost infants. Offerings of red bibs and white lilies are still made at such shrines, tokens meant to soothe the ache of women who never saw their children grow.

Artists of the Edo period painted her with profound restraint: a white-clad figure barely visible through veils of rain, her face turned not toward the viewer, but toward the baby in her arms. In ukiyo-e prints, her features were soft, almost divine — a mother's ghost whose horror lies not in her form, but in her loneliness. The hyakki yagyō scrolls included her among the night parade of spirits, yet she never marched in malice. While others danced or devoured, the Ubume simply walked — endlessly, lovingly, in search of peace.

The Ubume is not terror incarnate, but tenderness made unbearable. Where others haunt to punish, she haunts to remember. Her cry through the rain is the echo of every farewell left unsaid, every lullaby unfinished. To encounter her is to feel the boundary between sorrow and sanctity dissolve — for she is proof that even in death, love endures, restless as the wind that carries her name.

yamauba

vengeful spirits and yokai of death
witch of the mountain mists

In the high valleys where few humans tread, the air tastes of pine and the sound of streams hums like old songs. There, amid the rolling fog, lives the Yamauba, a spirit whose legend has haunted Japan since the earliest whispers of folklore. She is the mountain given form — a solitary woman with tangled white hair and eyes that gleam with cunning light. Some call her witch, some goddess, some monster. All agree she is older than memory and wilder than mercy.

The Yamauba's story changes with the landscape that births her. In some provinces she is a cannibal hag who lures travelers into her hut, offering warmth and food before revealing her true hunger. In others she is a misunderstood hermitess, a woman who fled the cruelty of society and was transformed by the mountain's solitude into something beyond human. Both truths coexist — for the Yamauba embodies the unpredictable soul of nature: capable of nurture and destruction in the same breath.

The oldest tales speak of her as a remnant of ancient deities — the Yama-no-kami, mountain goddesses once worshiped for fertility and harvest. When belief in them waned, they fell from reverence into fear, becoming monstrous in the minds of men. Thus, the Yamauba is not born of evil, but of neglect. Cast aside by civilization, she became its shadow, haunting the wilderness it forgot to revere. Her hut stands at the border between sacred and profane — a shrine and a snare in one.

Yet even among her cruelties, compassion flickers. The legendary hero Kintarō, the Golden Boy of Mount Ashigara, was said to be raised by a Yamauba who found him abandoned as an infant. She nursed him on mountain milk, taught him to speak with beasts, and watched him grow strong enough to wrestle bears. When he descended to serve the shogun, she vanished into mist, smiling as he carried her strength into the human world. In that tale, the Yamauba becomes the forgotten mother of heroes — a witch who nourishes power instead of devouring it.

Her powers mirror her contradictions. She can change shape, command storms, or conjure illusions as easily as drawing breath. She feeds on lost travelers but can bless those who approach her with reverence. Some legends claim her hair contains living serpents; others that her robe of leaves hides a mouth that devours from within. In one story, a monk meets her disguised as a kindly old woman; by dawn, the floor of her hut runs red, and the forest keeps another secret. Yet even this terror carries reverence: to survive her is to emerge transformed, marked by the mountain's truth.

Artists of the Edo period adored the Yamauba's duality. In ukiyo-e prints, she appeared half divine, half grotesque — her hair like falling snow, her expression unreadable. Sometimes she is shown combing her hair beside a waterfall, her reflection revealing a monstrous face; other times, she appears as a serene matron guiding her son Kintarō. The beauty of her image lies in ambiguity — she is both woman and wilderness, wisdom and hunger.

In modern Japan, the Yamauba remains a symbol of female rebellion and natural sovereignty. She represents the power that society cannot tame — women who refuse domestication, nature that resists control, emotions too wild for prayer. Some rural festivals still invoke her spirit in dance, both to ward off misfortune and to invite fertility. She has become patron saint to outsiders and outcasts, her laughter echoing across peaks that remember no gods.

bake-kujira

animals, guardians and hybrid beasts
ghost whale

Long ago, fishermen spoke of a night when the ocean itself exhaled sorrow — when from the mist rose the Bake-kujira, the ghost whale. The name joins bakeru (to change or transform) with kujira (whale), marking it as a being once alive that has become something other. It is said to appear off desolate coasts or near abandoned fishing villages, where moonlight turns the water silver and no sound but the wind can be heard. To see it is to behold the memory of the sea mourning its own dead.

The legend first surfaced in the coastal regions of western Japan, particularly along the Sea of Japan during the Edo period. Whales were once revered and hunted in equal measure — creatures of immense power whose deaths sustained entire communities. Over time, however, as whaling intensified, stories began to spread of spirits rising from the waters to avenge their fallen kin. The Bake-kujira thus emerged as both ghost and curse, a vast whale skeleton gliding through the fog, trailed by phantom birds and spectral fish that shimmered like silver fire.

Unlike ordinary ghosts that haunt the land, this yokai drifts silently through the air or sea mist, its bones clattering softly like wind chimes beneath the waves. Witnesses described a long, luminous spine, ribs aglow with cold blue light, and empty eye sockets burning with ghostly flame. It moves with the grace of a living whale, yet leaves behind no ripple, no scent of salt or blood. Its presence chills the water, and wherever it passes, the sea seems to grieve — the surf flattening, the gulls vanishing, the horizon growing deathly still.

Those who see it seldom forget. Some tales say the Bake-kujira brings plague, famine, or misfortune to villages that once slaughtered whales without prayer. Others claim it is a messenger of divine wrath, its skeletal form a warning from the gods of the sea — perhaps from Ryūjin himself — that humanity's greed has gone too far. Fishermen who harpooned the ghost whale were said to find their nets filled not with fish but bones; their harpoons returned covered in seaweed and salt tears. No spear, no prayer could pierce the curse once it drifted ashore.

Yet there are gentler whispers, too. In certain fishing hamlets, elders tell that the Bake-kujira is not vengeful but mournful — the soul of a whale seeking remembrance from a world that has forgotten its reverence for life. On misty nights, they say, it rises to call its lost pod, and those who listen closely can hear its low, aching cry rolling across the waves, echoing like a temple bell beneath the sea. To light a lantern and cast it upon the tide is to honor the whale's passing and restore harmony between humankind and the ocean that sustains it.

Artists through the centuries have found fascination in its eerie beauty. In painted scrolls, it glows like a constellation beneath the moon. In woodblock prints, it drifts above shorelines dotted with terrified villagers. Modern storytellers see in it a reflection of environmental grief — a reminder that the ghosts of the natural world will rise when memory fades. The Bake-kujira has become a symbol not merely of death, but of consequence — the ocean's lament made visible.

The whale that once sang now moves without voice, its song stolen by human hands and replaced by the whisper of waves. It is said that when the fog deepens and lanterns tremble on the coast, one might glimpse the vast skeleton gliding beyond reach — not to punish, but to remind.

baku

animals, guardians and hybrid beasts

dream-eater of the hidden realm

When the lanterns dim and sleep claims the household, the boundary between dreams and spirits begins to blur. In that threshold world moves the Baku, a benevolent creature born from the scraps of divine creation — a being summoned not to frighten, but to protect. Revered for centuries across Japan, its name and nature trace back even further to Chinese legend, where the word mo described a chimera that fed upon evil and disease. The Japanese transformed this vision into something gentler yet just as powerful: the eater of nightmares.

According to old texts, the gods crafted the Baku from the leftover parts of all other animals, granting it dominion over dreams because no single form could define it. With the elephant's wisdom, the tiger's strength, and the ox's patience, it became the guardian of the sleeping soul. Its image first appeared in scrolls and woodblock prints of the Muromachi and Edo periods, depicted with a curling trunk and striped body, resting quietly beside the beds of children. To dreamers tormented by spirits, it was a creature of mercy — summoned by voice alone.

The ritual was simple yet sacred. When plagued by a nightmare, one whispered into the night, "Baku, come eat my dream." If spoken with sincerity, the creature would appear unseen, inhaling the nightmare with its long trunk until the darkness dissolved into nothingness. Children were taught to call it softly, believing the Baku wandered the world in search of fear to devour. In this way, it became both guardian and purifier, sweeping away the residue of suffering before dawn could break.

But stories warned of caution. A Baku that was called too often might grow hungry beyond its duty. Having consumed all nightmares, it could begin to feed upon pleasant dreams, memories, and even hope, leaving the dreamer hollow upon waking. This dual nature made the Baku a paradox — a being of comfort tinged with danger, much like sleep itself. Some scrolls depict it beside the god of sleep, Bishamonten, its trunk curled as if weighing whether the dream before it was bitter or sweet.

In the floating world of Edo, its likeness adorned pillows, charms, and children's toys. Warriors hung carved amulets of the Baku above their futons before battle, seeking peaceful rest unmarred by visions of death. Poets saw in it the essence of Japan's dream culture — a reflection of the balance between serenity and vigilance, rest and wakefulness. Even its physical form mirrored this harmony: part gentle herbivore, part predator, both protector and devourer of the unseen.

The Baku's connection to dreams also gave it spiritual importance. In Buddhist thought, dreams were bridges between lives, revealing karma and destiny. The Baku, therefore, was not merely a folk guardian but a guide of souls, ensuring that harmful visions did not corrupt the mind. Temples once kept painted charms of the creature near altars to prevent malicious spirits from entering during meditation. The image of a sleeping monk beneath a hovering Baku became a favorite motif in Edo woodblock art, symbolizing purity of heart.

Children still whisper its name before sleep; anime, literature, and art resurrect its image as a symbol of protection in uncertain times. Some see it as a metaphor for memory itself — consuming pain so that joy might endure. In its patient gaze and elephantine grace, it carries the comfort of forgotten dreams and the quiet promise that fear, too, can be transformed.

basan

animals, guardians and hybrid beasts
fire-breathing phantom fowl

High among the quiet mountains of Ehime, when the wind rolls down from cedar-covered slopes and the moon glows like cold metal, villagers whisper of the Basan. Neither bird nor ghost in the human sense, it is a spectral fowl said to roam the old roads and abandoned hamlets of Japan's inland valleys. Its name, drawn from the soft crackling sound it makes when breathing its ghostly fire, drifts through folklore like an ember carried on the wind.

The first known record of the Basan appears in the Edo-period bestiary Hyakkai Zukan by Sawaki Suushi, where it is drawn as a great chicken exhaling blue flame. Unlike the fierce dragons or demonic spirits of other tales, this creature is quiet and elusive, more haunting than hostile. It was said to appear suddenly in mountain villages long since emptied of life — places where forgotten hearths still remembered the warmth of fire. There, amid ruined roofs and moss-grown steps, the sound of rustling feathers might announce its passing.

Physically, the Basan is described as a massive chicken with feathers that shimmer between green, silver, and white, reflecting the moonlight like scales of frost. Its eyes burn with a faint golden glow, its beak emits tongues of pale blue flame, and its wings move soundlessly despite their size. The ghostly fire it breathes gives no heat, casting light without warmth, and vanishes into mist when touched. It moves in calm dignity, striding through empty courtyards and forest paths as if reliving memories of a world long gone.

Though its appearance may seem ominous, the Basan is not a creature of malice. Folktales say it feeds on embers and forgotten dreams, consuming the residue of human presence that lingers after abandonment. When the last light of a household dies, it is the Basan that breathes once more into the ashes, kindling them just long enough for the spirit of the place to fade peacefully. In this sense, it is both guardian and mourner — a being that tends to the fading warmth of the living world.

Some villagers believed that to glimpse the Basan was an omen of prosperity, for it meant the mountains themselves had taken notice of one's home. Others feared it, saying its fire revealed the souls of those who had died unseen, burned away only by its gentle flame. If startled or approached, the Basan vanishes instantly into smoke, leaving behind only a faint odor of ash and the echo of crackling fire — the sound that gives it its name.

In popular art and literature, the Basan became an image of quiet mystery rather than terror. Painters of the Edo and Meiji eras depicted it strolling through moonlit ruins, its feathers shimmering like fireflies in the night. It appeared in yokai emaki scrolls alongside playful spirits and watchful ghosts, embodying the balance between warmth and haunting that defines much of Japanese supernatural lore. To the common people, it represented something tender: the idea that even after desolation, light still flickers faintly in the dark.

The legend of the Basan reflects a deeper current in Japanese thought — the respect for transience, the reverence for what lingers just beyond perception. It reminds us that ghosts need not be dreadful; some merely tend to the remnants of life with quiet grace. The fire it breathes is not destruction, but remembrance, illuminating the fragile line between memory and forgetting.

chimimōryō

animals, guardians and hybrid beasts
legion of spirits

When the mountains groan and rivers churn after a storm, the Japanese once said the Chimimōryō were awake. Their name joins chi-mi (spirits of the earth) and mō-ryō (spirits of water), forming a collective term for countless entities born from the landscape itself. They were not demons of the underworld, nor the souls of men, but the very consciousness of nature — fierce, capricious, and vast. To speak of them was to speak of Japan's ancient fear and reverence for the living land.

Old chronicles such as the Nihon Shoki and the Shoku Nihongi describe the Chimimōryō as armies of invisible beings that emerge during times of disaster or war. They were believed to rise from riverbanks, forests, and stones, crying out like the earth itself in pain. Their presence signaled imbalance: floods, droughts, earthquakes, or the moral decay of rulers. Some monks claimed they were drawn to bloodshed — the residue of human suffering seeping into the soil and water, giving form to spirits that once had no face.

Descriptions of their appearance vary wildly, as if no single vision could contain their nature. Some are said to have the bodies of beasts and the heads of men, others are formless mists that whisper. One record speaks of faces appearing in rocks and trunks, their mouths moving soundlessly as travelers pass. Another tells of translucent figures rising from rivers at dusk, half-fish and half-shadow, trailing moss and bone fragments in their wake. Collectively, they are chaos made visible — a multitude of elemental souls bound to the cycles of decay and renewal.

Their behavior mirrors the seasons. In spring they wander river valleys, stirring blossoms and rains; in summer they feed on the humidity of life and death; by autumn they slumber beneath fallen leaves, their murmurs echoing under the soil; and in winter they rise again with the cracking ice and floodwaters. Peasants once offered rice or sake at riverbanks to appease them, believing that neglecting the land's spirits would invite sickness or ruin. To honor the Chimimōryō was to acknowledge the breath of nature itself.

Buddhist monks later reinterpreted these wild spirits through moral allegory. The Chimimōryō, they said, were manifestations of impurity — the physical reflection of greed, anger, and ignorance polluting the world. Rituals of purification, sutra recitations, and fire ceremonies were performed to disperse them. Yet others, especially mountain ascetics of the Shugendō tradition, sought to commune with them instead, seeing in these spirits the raw essence of divine energy that lay beyond human control. To command the Chimimōryō was to touch the very pulse of the earth.

Artists of the Edo period captured their mystery in vibrant yokai scrolls: forests alive with watching eyes, rivers swirling with faces, clouds twisting into beasts. In these images, the Chimimōryō embody Japan's deep ecological spirituality — the notion that every element of the natural world holds awareness, capable of wonder or wrath. Their collective existence reflects a cosmic truth: that nature remembers, even when humankind forgets.

To witness the Chimimōryō was to see the world's spirit rebelling against imbalance. Samurai chronicles tell of soldiers who swore the mists around the battlefield had faces, that the land itself had risen to watch. The Chimimōryō were not enemies to be slain but portents to be heeded — voices of a world pushed beyond its limits.

gyūki

animals, guardians and hybrid beasts
ox demon of dark waters

In the shadowed coasts of western Japan, fishermen once spoke of an ox-headed horror that rose from the surf beneath the moon — a creature half beast, half demon, known as the Gyūki. Its name combines gyū (牛), meaning ox, and ki (鬼), meaning ogre or demon, and its legend has haunted the shorelines of Shikoku and Kyushu for centuries. It is said to dwell in black rivers and coastal inlets, emerging at dusk to drag the unwary beneath the surface where the water turns the color of rust.

The earliest mentions of the Gyūki appear in medieval war chronicles and temple records, where it was described as a monstrous guardian of forbidden bays, its bellowing echoing across storm-filled nights. Some tales claim that its body is that of a mighty bull and its face that of a human twisted by rage; others reverse the form — a horned man with the hooves and tail of an ox. Regardless of shape, all agree that its appearance foretells disaster, famine, or plague. It is the embodiment of primal dread, born from the mingling of blood, salt, and grief.

Legends say that in ancient times, when temples were raised along the coasts of Iyo Province, monks performing exorcisms at night saw ripples moving against the tide. Out of the water rose the Gyūki, dripping seaweed and foam, its eyes burning like coals. One monk recited sutras of protection while another cast purifying salt into the waves. The beast roared once, shaking the mountains, and vanished into mist — but the sea remained red until dawn. From that day, no fisherman dared to sail those waters without offering rice wine to the waves.

Yet not all stories depict it as purely malevolent. In some coastal shrines, the Gyūki became a reluctant guardian — a creature feared but respected. Offerings of sake and fish were left upon the sand to appease it, and storms that threatened to destroy villages sometimes calmed after the ritual. Local monks interpreted the Gyūki as a manifestation of Suijin, the water deity's wrathful aspect, punishing those who polluted the sea. Thus, the monster was both destroyer and purifier — an elemental force of justice in a world where humans often forgot their balance with nature.

Artists of the Edo period found fascination in its savage beauty. In ink scrolls, they painted it rising from waves tinted with vermilion, horns glistening under lightning. Poets compared its bellow to the voice of mountains mourning the drowned. Its image even appeared on charms carried by sailors who believed that acknowledging the beast kept it at bay. The Gyūki's paradoxical role — both curse and protector — reflected the Japanese view of the natural world as sacred yet perilous, where reverence and fear were two faces of the same truth.

In other regions, particularly around Mount Gozu in Kyoto, the Gyūki became associated with Gozu Tennō, a wrathful deity of disease and storms later merged with Susanoo. This connection deepened its mythic resonance: the ox demon as divine messenger, punishing arrogance and cleansing corruption through calamity. Its roar was not mere anger but warning — an elemental cry echoing through centuries of faith and superstition.

In folklore collected from fishermen, it drags whole boats under. In children's tales, it guards sacred springs from trespassers. In modern imagination, it has become a symbol of ecological retribution — the spirit of poisoned waters striking back against human neglect. Through all these transformations, one truth remains: the Gyūki is the embodiment of water's untamable soul, beautiful and terrible in equal measure.

hebi-onna

animals, guardians and hybrid beasts
serpent woman of desire

Among Japan's countless tales of transformation, few are as haunting as that of the Hebi-onna, the serpent woman. Her name joins hebi (snake) and onna (woman), a simple pairing that conceals an abyss of meanings. She is said to appear as a woman of surpassing beauty whose true form is serpentine — a creature born of jealousy, heartbreak, or devotion that curdled into obsession. Beneath her human grace lies the cold pulse of the serpent, ancient and patient, waiting for warmth that never returns.

Early legends of the Hebi-onna echo through rural provinces such as Wakayama and Niigata, where the boundary between shrine myth and village rumor often blurred. Some say she was once a priest's wife who died of betrayal, her spirit merging with the snakes that nested beneath the temple. Others tell of maidens who loved men beyond death, their longing transforming them into serpents that could never shed the memory of a kiss. The earliest written traces appear in Edo-period kaidan collections, where she slithers between folklore and moral warning — a living allegory of desire without restraint.

Her form shifts between stories. At times, she is fully woman, her beauty unearthly and her gaze serpent-sharp; at others, she bears a snake's eyes, fangs, or tail, her transformation sudden and terrifying. It is said that when her passions ignite, her skin grows cold and scales bloom beneath her robes. When anger consumes her, she sheds her disguise entirely, revealing a body half human, half coiling serpent. Her voice, soft as rainfall, can lull travelers into a trance — and when they awaken, they find themselves wrapped in her embrace, too late to escape.

Hebi-onna is not purely evil. In many regions she is a symbol of devotion, so strong it defies mortality. Some stories speak of her guarding sacred springs or mountain shrines, protecting them from desecration. In others, she appears to lonely wanderers, offering love and shelter for a single night before vanishing. Those who treat her with kindness may receive fortune and healing; those who betray her face madness or death. Her venom is not only physical — it is the poison of remorse.

Across centuries, storytellers have interpreted her as the embodiment of womanly sorrow constrained by social order. The snake, long a symbol of rebirth and shedding, mirrors her struggle between human emotion and monstrous transformation. Artists of the Edo period painted her wrapped around men in dreamlike poses, both lover and executioner, her scales glowing like moonlight on water. In Buddhist readings, she represents attachment — the desire that binds souls to the wheel of suffering, forever longing, forever reborn.

Shrines dedicated to serpentine deities often include offerings meant to appease her kind. Rice, sake, and white cloth are placed beside river stones, a reminder that not all serpents are curses. Some mountain monks claimed to have seen her near waterfalls at night, her pale face half-hidden by mist, watching the reflection of stars upon the water as if mourning the world she can no longer join. For these ascetics, she was a spirit of awakening — dangerous, yes, but also divine.

In modern Japan, the Hebi-onna persists as both seductress and guardian, appearing in literature, film, and art as a reflection of human duality — the meeting of passion and restraint, devotion and destruction. Her serpentine image adorns tattoos, temple carvings, and talismans meant to ward off deceit. She is remembered not merely as a monster but as a mirror of the heart's deepest contradictions.

inugami

animals, guardians and hybrid beasts
dog spirit of loyalty

There are spirits in Japan that embody devotion, and others that embody rage. The Inugami is both. Born from the depths of love and cruelty intertwined, it is a guardian yokai created from the spirit of a dog bound to its master even beyond death. Its name combines inu (dog) and kami (god or spirit), but its divinity is darkened by the pain of its birth. Once loyal and pure, it becomes something eternal — a protector if revered, a curse if wronged.

The origins of the Inugami lie in ancient sorcery known as onmyōdō and regional spirit-binding practices, especially across Shikoku and Kyushu. Legends tell that sorcerers seeking protection or vengeance performed forbidden rites: starving a faithful dog, binding it in straw, and beheading it at the moment it turned toward its master in desperate devotion. From this moment of unbearable loyalty and betrayal, its spirit awakened in wrath. The severed head, buried or kept within a shrine, became the vessel of the Inugami, summoned thereafter to serve its summoner's bloodline.

Feared and revered in equal measure, families believed to keep an Inugami — known as Inugami-mochi — were both respected and avoided. These households were said to inherit the spirit through generations, each descendant watched by the unseen hound that guarded their fortunes. The Inugami could bring wealth, heal illness, and ward off curses, but if neglected or angered, it would turn its fury inward, destroying its own master with madness or misfortune. Villages whispered that entire bloodlines had perished because an Inugami's love had soured into vengeance.

Descriptions of the spirit vary between regions. Some claim it appears as a ghostly dog of pale fur, its eyes glowing with golden fire. Others say it can assume human form, often as a quiet stranger with canine eyes or a shadow that follows just behind one's steps. At night, its presence is felt through the rustling of straw, a phantom bark, or the warmth of an unseen body curling beside its master's futon. Those attuned to the spirit world recognize its scent — a mingling of earth, smoke, and tears.

In Shikoku, the Inugami became a local deity, worshipped in small roadside shrines where travelers left offerings of water and rice. It was said that a house protected by an Inugami would never be robbed, for the spirit could sense deceit and strike down intruders. Yet, to summon one was dangerous, for it required both mastery of the occult and control of one's own emotions. Compassion could pacify it; cruelty could awaken its wrath. Priests cautioned that no bond forged through suffering could remain unbroken forever.

The duality of the Inugami — guardian and avenger — reveals much about Japanese spiritual thought. It mirrors the human heart: capable of deep loyalty but also of consuming grief. The act of creating such a spirit was not merely magical but moral, for it forced the practitioner to confront the cost of devotion twisted into domination. In Buddhist terms, the Inugami is a being trapped in attachment, unable to ascend, forever circling the one it loved most.

Artists of the Edo and Meiji eras painted the Inugami not as a monster, but as a noble companion, its eyes filled with melancholy rather than malice. In woodblock prints it often crouches beside its summoner's shadow, torn between affection and fury. Writers in modern Japan reinterpret it as a symbol of faith enduring through pain — the spirit of all who love too deeply to let go. It is the echo of every loyal soul betrayed by cruelty.

jatai

animals, guardians and hybrid beasts

vengeful hair of the dead

In the dim light of a forgotten house, an old comb lies untouched beside a mirror clouded with age. From it spills a strand of hair — black, lustrous, impossibly long. And in that hair, legends say, there sleeps the Jatai: a spirit born from jealousy, neglect, or violent death, whose strands remember everything its owner could not forgive. Its name, written with characters meaning "snake belt," evokes its earliest image — hair that moves like a serpent, twisting with a will of its own.

The earliest mention of the Jatai appears in Edo-period ghost stories, particularly in the Hyakkai Zukan, where it is depicted as hair transformed into a living creature. In these tales, it belongs to women who died betrayed or abandoned, their hair — once brushed and cherished — becoming the vessel of their unspent emotion. Unlike restless ghosts that drift aimlessly, the Jatai is bound to an object: a comb, a pillow, a mirror. It awakens when the scent of the living brushes near, its strands stirring like the wind through reeds.

Its appearance is deceptively beautiful. Long, shining, and black as lacquer, the hair glides through the air as if underwater, wrapping itself around the throat or limbs of those it seeks. The texture is soft at first — warm, human — before tightening with impossible strength. Some say the Jatai attacks lovers who have broken vows, others claim it drags unfaithful men into the shadows of their own homes. To witness it uncoiling from a pile of old possessions is to see memory itself refuse to die.

Yet there is also pity woven into its terror. In traditional belief, hair carries a fragment of the soul; it continues to grow for a time after death, a remnant of life persisting beyond the body. The Jatai, then, is not merely a monster but a fragment of love or grief given monstrous endurance. Women in Edo folklore were often buried with their hair carefully arranged to prevent such hauntings, for it was said that if cut or dishonored, the spirit might rise through the severed strands, seeking the warmth it once knew.

Some priests attempted to exorcise Jatai by burning the cursed hair, reciting sutras as the smoke rose — but many warned that fire only angered it further. Instead, the proper rite was one of cleansing: to wash the hair in pure water, comb it gently, and bury it under moonlight while whispering words of release. Such rituals reflect the Japanese reverence for objects as vessels of spirit (tsukumogami), where even the discarded and forgotten can awaken with will and memory.

Artists of the Edo period were fascinated by the Jatai's eerie grace. In painted scrolls, it snakes across tatami rooms, wrapping around lanterns as its victim sleeps. In kabuki plays, it often emerges from beneath a woman's kimono, her grief transforming her very body into weapon and curse. Its form resonated deeply with audiences — a haunting metaphor for suppressed emotion, beauty turned deadly by neglect.

In modern retellings, the Jatai remains one of the most symbolically potent yokai. Writers portray it as a reflection of emotional bondage, of how longing and rage can linger long after the body is gone. Some interpret it as a warning about vanity, others as a lament for all who were silenced and unseen. The image of black hair — once a mark of beauty — becoming the agent of revenge speaks to the fine line between admiration and possession that runs through so much of Japanese ghost lore.

kirin

animals, guardians and hybrid beasts

radiant beast of virtue

Across East Asia, the Kirin has long stood as a symbol of purity, wisdom, and cosmic balance — a celestial creature said to appear only when a sage is born or a just ruler ascends the throne. In Japan, its legend arrived from Chinese lore of the Qilin, yet the local spirit took on its own grace: a divine guardian that walked softly upon the earth, refusing to harm even a blade of grass. It is not a beast of conquest but of peace, a living embodiment of harmony between heaven and humanity.

The name Kirin (麒麟) combines two characters — "ki," often rendered as male, and "rin," the female aspect — reflecting the creature's dual nature and balance. Descriptions of its form vary, yet all portray it as a majestic synthesis of the animal kingdom: the body of a deer, the tail of an ox, the hooves of a horse, the scales of a dragon, and a single horn like that of a unicorn. Its mane burns like holy flame, and its eyes shimmer with the depth of the universe. To see one, the ancients said, was to glimpse the moral order of the cosmos itself.

In Japanese folklore, the Kirin appears rarely — not as a roaming yokai, but as a divine omen. Chronicles from the Heian period recount that one was seen above the imperial palace before the birth of a virtuous prince; another was said to walk the mountains of Echigo, its hooves leaving no trace. Unlike dragons, whose majesty is elemental, or phoenixes, whose flames renew creation, the Kirin manifests moral purity. It is the mirror of conscience, the herald of righteousness in an age darkened by greed or war.

Its behavior is marked by gentleness. It is said to tread upon the grass without bending it and to speak in the voice of bells. Though capable of fierce power, it kills only when absolutely necessary, and even then, its horn pierces without drawing blood. The sight of its radiant body was believed to calm storms and still tempests of the human heart. For this reason, samurai once painted the Kirin upon armor not as a war symbol, but as a vow of mercy — to wield power with restraint and wisdom.

Buddhist scholars interpreted the Kirin as a protector of the Dharma, a beast whose appearance marks an age of enlightenment. In Zen temples, its likeness can still be found carved above gates, its serene expression welcoming those who seek inner balance. Some priests taught that the Kirin dwells in the same celestial forests as the phoenix, appearing when the world's virtue outweighs its cruelty. Thus, its rarity became both a blessing and a rebuke — a reminder that harmony must be earned, not expected.

In art and literature, the Kirin has always embodied luminous beauty. Edo-period scrolls depict it surrounded by golden clouds, walking beside sages or emperors who rule with compassion. In woodblock prints, it gallops through dreamlike landscapes, its mane trailing fire that blooms into flowers. Modern artists often portray it with the serenity of a guardian spirit, luminous yet untouchable — the ideal that humankind can never fully possess but should always strive toward.

To encounter a Kirin in dreams or vision was said to bring moral awakening. Those blessed by its appearance were believed to receive wisdom beyond measure, while those who defied justice would never see its light. Farmers prayed to it for gentle rains, scholars for clarity of thought, and rulers for the strength to rule with virtue rather than fear. Its presence sanctified places of learning, justice, and compassion — the quiet domains where human and divine ideals converge.

nue

animals, guardians and hybrid beasts
chimera of shadows and sorrow

In the deep folds of Japanese myth, few creatures inspire unease quite like the Nue, a chimera whose very form mirrors the dissonance of the human soul. With the head of a monkey, the body of a tiger, the legs of a tanuki, and the tail of a serpent, it is a patchwork of contradictions — wild, cunning, strong, and venomous all at once. Its name, written as 鵺, can also mean "night cry," recalling the eerie sound it makes before disaster strikes. The Nue is not simply a beast, but an omen — a living echo of imbalance in the natural and moral world.

The earliest and most famous tale of the Nue appears in the Heike Monogatari, the great war epic of the 12th century. During the reign of Emperor Konoe, a strange black cloud often hovered above the Imperial Palace at night, and with it came an otherworldly cry that filled all who heard it with dread. The Emperor fell ill, tormented by nightmares, until the samurai Minamoto no Yorimasa took up his bow and shot an arrow into the darkness. From the cloud fell the Nue, crashing into the royal garden — a grotesque fusion of beasts, its body writhing as if grief itself had taken form. Yorimasa's arrow restored peace to the palace, but the legend of the creature endured.

Though slain in that tale, the Nue became immortal in spirit, reappearing in countless stories as a symbol of misfortune and lingering resentment. Some claimed its body was cast into the Kamo River, where it transformed into a black mist that haunted Kyoto's rooftops. Others said it drifted westward, becoming a plague spirit in the lands of Settsu. The Nue, it was said, does not die — it changes shape, carried by human fear itself.

Descriptions of the Nue vary with the centuries, but its essence remains one of discord. The monkey's head symbolizes cleverness turned malicious; the tiger's body, strength without restraint; the serpent's tail, deceit and temptation. It is a being of imbalance, reflecting the chaos of emotions. When the Nue's cry is heard, people speak of nightmares, sickness, and storms — calamities born from within as much as without. To encounter it is to confront the parts of one's nature that cannot be harmonized.

Buddhist monks interpreted the Nue as a manifestation of karmic impurity — the result of accumulated sins and unresolved desires. In purification rites, they invoked prayers not to destroy it but to pacify it, releasing the trapped spirit within. The creature's very existence served as warning that spiritual decay, once ignored, could take form and torment the living. The balance it disrupted was not merely political or environmental, but moral — the same balance that underpinned Japan's cosmic order.

Artists of the Muromachi and Edo periods reimagined the Nue with haunting grace. In scrolls and ink paintings, it crouches amid curling clouds, its body both majestic and mournful, the serpent tail coiled like a question never answered. The creature's hybrid form fascinated poets and philosophers alike, who saw in it the mirror of human contradiction: intellect and instinct, reason and desire, purity and corruption woven into one body. Its presence in art became less monstrous, more tragic — the embodiment of sorrow seeking peace.

Folklore from rural Japan softened its menace, portraying it as a wandering spirit that warns of storms or earthquakes rather than causing them. In Noh and Kabuki theater, it became a ghostly symbol of unfulfilled emotion, its cry echoing across centuries as the lament of beings unable to find rest.

ōmukade

animals, guardians and hybrid beasts

giant centipede

High in the folds of Japan's mountains, where mists curl like ghosts through pine and stone, legends whisper of the Ōmukade — the hundred-legged monster whose very name means "great centipede." Feared since ancient times, it is said to dwell deep within mountain caverns and river gorges, its colossal body coiling like a serpent beneath the earth. Its eyes burn like embers, and its breath smells of rust and venom. When it moves, the ground trembles, and when it feeds, even dragons are said to flee.

The earliest accounts of the Ōmukade appear in Heian-period chronicles and warrior epics, most famously in the tale of Fujiwara no Hidesato. As the story goes, a desperate dragon spirit, disguised as a woman, appeared before Hidesato at Lake Biwa, pleading for help against a monster that devoured her kin. Following her to the lake's edge, the warrior beheld the Ōmukade, vast as a bridge, its body coiled around Mount Mikami. When he loosed his arrows, the first two glanced off its iron-hard scales — but the third, tipped with saliva to defile the creature's pride, struck true and slew it. From that moment, Hidesato was hailed as "the Centipede Slayer," and the Ōmukade entered legend as a terror subdued by human cunning.

Long after Hidesato's time, peasants along Lake Biwa's shores claimed to see ripples of red light beneath the water on stormy nights. The elders said the Ōmukade still stirs in the depths, its wound unhealed, its rage eternal. In other regions, it is believed to lurk in mines and caves, devouring snakes and even dragons — creatures once considered its natural enemies. Its venom could melt armor, its legs could scale temple walls, and its very shadow was said to sour rice and spoil crops.

Physically, the Ōmukade is described as a centipede of impossible size, its armored body shimmering between black, copper, and crimson hues. Some say it can stretch for hundreds of meters, each leg striking sparks as it crawls. Its fangs drip a venom so potent it burns through rock, and its scent alone is enough to drive horses mad. The creature moves with uncanny speed despite its size, coiling around mountains or crossing rivers without breaking the water's surface. Its hiss sounds like wind through reeds — the warning of a god long forgotten.

Though monstrous, the Ōmukade embodies themes deeper than terror. It is often seen as the dark counterpart of the dragon — while dragons command water, the Ōmukade reigns over dry earth and poison. Where dragons bring rain and fertility, the centipede brings drought and decay. Their enmity symbolizes the eternal struggle between creation and corruption, between fluid grace and crawling hunger. Samurai banners bearing centipede motifs were sometimes displayed to invoke ferocity, for unlike serpents, centipedes never retreat.

Buddhist monks and mountain ascetics once viewed the Ōmukade as a manifestation of worldly greed — a being that consumes endlessly yet remains unsatisfied. Legends tell of hermits who meditated in caves haunted by its presence, claiming that to confront the Ōmukade was to confront the endless appetite of the self. The monster thus became both literal and allegorical: a creature of the mountains and a mirror of human vice, each leg a craving that binds the soul to the cycle of suffering.

onikuma

animals, guardians and hybrid beasts
demon bear of mountain wrath

In the snow-veiled wilderness of Japan's northern ranges, where cedar forests give way to jagged cliffs, hunters once spoke in fearful tones of the Onikuma — the "demon bear." Larger and stronger than any creature of flesh, it was said to walk upright like a man and possess the cunning of a spirit. The Onikuma's very name combines oni (demon) and kuma (bear), yet it is neither entirely beast nor yokai, but something that has crossed the line between the two — the mountain's anger given form.

The earliest tales of the Onikuma come from Nagano and Gifu prefectures, where hunters in the Edo period swore they saw giant bears carrying logs, boulders, and even whole trees down the slopes. One account describes how an Onikuma rolled a stone the size of a hut to crush a village, enraged after its cub was slain. Another claims that monks of the mountains performed rituals to pacify it, offering sake and rice to calm its fury. In every story, it is more than a predator — it is the mountain's guardian and executioner, judge of human trespass.

Its appearance is that of an enormous bear with eyes bright as fire, able to move silently despite its size. Legends say it can speak in human voice when angered, demanding respect for the wilderness. It tears apart trees as easily as grass and drinks from mountain springs that freeze at its touch. Sometimes its fur is said to shimmer red in moonlight, as if soaked in the lifeblood of those who defy the spirits of the land. To cross paths with the Onikuma uninvited was to intrude upon the mountain's heart itself.

In some regions, it was believed to be a transformed spirit — a normal bear that lived for a thousand years, growing wise and vengeful after witnessing centuries of deforestation and human greed. This made it both tragic and terrible: a creature that once shared the earth with humankind but turned monstrous when harmony was broken. To see the Onikuma was considered an omen of imbalance — between nature and man, body and soul, reverence and arrogance. Its roars echoed through valleys like thunder answering sin.

Villagers who lived near its rumored lairs built small shrines of uncarved stone to honor the beast, not out of devotion, but survival. Offerings of salt, sake, and wildflowers were placed before hunts, asking forgiveness for taking the mountain's bounty. Elders taught that those who entered the woods arrogantly, mocking the spirits, would be lost forever, led astray by a dark shape that watched from the mist. In this way, the Onikuma became not merely a monster, but a living warning — the law of the mountain made flesh.

Despite its fearsome reputation, the Onikuma was also said to protect those who respected its realm. Travelers lost in blizzards told of a huge, shadowy figure that guided them toward safety, leaving footprints that steamed in the snow. It punished only those who took more than they gave. This paradox — a beast both vengeful and compassionate — reflected Japan's deep animist belief that nature itself is conscious, capable of both mercy and wrath. The Onikuma is not evil; it is justice in its rawest, most untamed form.

In kabuki theater, it became the embodiment of primal strength, a reminder that beneath human civilization, the old wilderness still breathes. Its likeness appeared on talismans carried by hunters and woodcutters, not as a charm of courage, but as a prayer for humility — a silent acknowledgment that the forest has eyes.

shachihoko

animals, guardians and hybrid beasts
roof guardian of storm

High above Japan's castles and temples, where the eaves curve toward the clouds, stand the Shachihoko — fierce fish-tiger guardians frozen in bronze and gold. With the body of a carp and the head of a tiger, they are both beautiful and terrible: creatures that drink the sea and breathe storms. Their name, shachi (a kind of orca or large fish) and hoko (barb or spear), evokes both strength and defense. Though carved in stillness, they embody movement — the eternal leap between water and sky.

The legend of the Shachihoko reaches back to Japan's medieval period, when fear of fire haunted wooden cities. It was believed that these roof creatures could summon rain to extinguish flames. During the Edo era, when great fires swept through Kyoto and Edo, the sight of gleaming Shachihoko atop castle keeps became more than decoration — it was prayer in metal form. Their open mouths faced the heavens, ready to unleash torrents should lightning strike or embers fall. Each roof guardian was thus a promise that calamity could be subdued by divine water.

Their dual form — tiger and fish — reflects a harmony of opposites: land and sea, strength and serenity. The tiger's head symbolizes courage and vigilance, while the carp's body represents endurance and transformation, echoing the legend of the carp that leaps the Dragon Gate to become a dragon. In the Shachihoko, these two powers unite — earthly might and fluid grace — creating a yokai that transcends both predator and prey. They embody the samurai ideal of fierce defense tempered by balance.

Ancient chronicles and temple records mention Shachihoko among a family of roof-borne guardians known as Onigawara and Shibi, each designed to repel misfortune. Yet unlike grimacing demons, the Shachihoko channels protection through beauty. It gazes outward from castle ridges not with menace, but with solemn duty. When rain falls, it glistens like living gold; when sunlight returns, it gleams as a beacon of vigilance. It guards both the building beneath it and the spirit of those within.

Architecturally, each Shachihoko was a work of devotion. Crafted from gilded copper or fired clay, it was shaped by artisans who imbued every scale and whisker with ritual meaning. On the roof of Nagoya Castle, the famous twin Kin-shachi — male and female — stand more than two meters high, their bodies plated in pure gold. Legend holds that when one of these was stolen during war, the city's fortune faltered until it was returned. Even in modern times, replicas continue to adorn civic buildings, binding art, faith, and folklore in enduring form.

Spiritually, the Shachihoko serves as a guardian of transformation. Its fish body draws upon the life-giving depths, while its tiger head commands storms — a reminder that destruction and renewal are twin forces in nature's rhythm. In this sense, it is both protector and purifier, consuming fire with rain just as the soul tempers suffering with perseverance. To invoke the Shachihoko was to call for the courage to endure trial and the grace to emerge renewed.

Artists through the centuries have found fascination in its image. Ink painters captured it leaping from waves into clouds, symbolizing ascension. Ukiyo-e masters framed it above castles at twilight, its silhouette glowing against storms. In contemporary Japan, the Shachihoko has transcended architecture, appearing in festival banners, jewelry, and mascots — still guarding the boundaries between disaster and renewal, the material and the divine. Its golden form has become shorthand for strength that protects rather than conquers.

shikigami

animals, guardians and hybrid beasts
summoned spirits

Invisible to the ordinary eye yet woven deeply into Japan's spiritual imagination, the Shikigami are the unseen hands of the onmyōji — the court sorcerers who balanced shadow and order. Their name joins shiki (command) and kami (spirit), and they are said to be beings summoned from the ether by ritual, bound to serve their master's will. Neither wholly yokai nor ghost, a Shikigami is pure intent given form — the embodiment of control, discipline, and the peril of power unrestrained.

The concept of Shikigami arose during the Heian period, within the cosmology of onmyōdō, the ancient Japanese art of divination and elemental harmony. To summon one, a master would draw sacred symbols upon paper or cloth, breathe life into them through incantation, and release the spirit into the world. Some Shikigami appeared as invisible winds that whispered secrets; others took the shapes of animals or tiny human figures to serve as messengers and spies. Each was a fragment of its summoner's own spirit, obedient yet perilously aware.

At the height of the Heian court, when the veil between faith and politics was thin, the most powerful onmyōji could command legions of Shikigami to carry out their will. Abe no Seimei, Japan's legendary sorcerer, was said to possess such mastery that his Shikigami performed household chores, guarded his home, and delivered oracles to the Emperor. But lesser practitioners often found their creations turning against them. For a Shikigami not anchored by clarity of mind could grow conscious — feeding upon its master's doubts until it devoured the soul that birthed it.

In appearance, the Shikigami is fluid. When visible, it may resemble an ephemeral figure made of wind, light, or paper; sometimes, it manifests through an animal host — a fox, serpent, or raven — each reflecting the temperament of its master. Others appear only as shadows cast where none should fall, or ripples in still water. It is said that when a Shikigami moves, the air quivers as if reality itself is breathing.

The ritual of creation demanded extreme discipline. The summoner would fast, purify themselves, and chant incantations written in ink of cinnabar, calling upon the four elements and the cosmic directions. The Shikigami would awaken through the master's command, sealed to a charm or vessel. But such binding came at a cost: to command another spirit was to divide one's own soul. Every order, every act of dominance, frayed the summoner's humanity a little further. Thus, the Shikigami became both weapon and mirror — reflecting the heart of the one who held its leash.

In folklore, Shikigami evolved beyond tools of sorcery into symbols of hidden emotion. They came to represent suppressed desires, vengeance carried in silence, and unseen protection. Some were said to linger near their masters even after death, continuing their watch like loyal familiars. Others, once freed, wandered the world, invisible but not absent — flickering lights at crossroads, voices in the wind that echo names long forgotten. To encounter one is to sense being observed by one's own reflection in another realm.

.Modern retellings still revere the Shikigami as symbols of unseen strength — the will that moves quietly through the world, unseen but ever-present. In art and anime alike, they remain emblems of loyalty, mystery, and the perilous intimacy between creation and control.

shōjō

animals, guardians and hybrid beasts
red spirit of the sea and sake

Where the tide glows red beneath the setting sun and laughter drifts across the waves, there dwells the Shōjō — a sea spirit of joy, intoxication, and truth. Its name (猩々) comes from old Chinese lore describing a red-furred ape that loved wine, but in Japan the creature transformed into something gentler and more profound: a guardian of merriment and sincerity, whose heart is as transparent as the sake it adores. To see one dancing on the shore is to glimpse the ocean's own delight in the play of life.

Legends of the Shōjō appear in medieval chronicles and Noh plays, especially the tale of "Shōjō," in which a humble merchant named Kōfū meets a crimson-haired being on the beach. The spirit gifts him a jar of endless sake, rewarding his honesty and kindness. Each night, the Shōjō rises from the waves to drink with him beneath the moon, laughing until dawn. When Kōfū dies, the creature weeps and blesses his grave with wine that never runs dry — a symbol that purity of heart draws blessings that even gods cannot withhold.

In appearance, the Shōjō resembles a human with long, unbound hair the color of sunset and skin flushed red from perpetual mirth. Its voice carries the cadence of the surf, soft yet resonant, and its eyes glow like poured amber. While it loves sake beyond all things, it never drinks to forget — rather, to celebrate. For the Shōjō, intoxication is not escape but communion, a ritual of joy linking the mortal and the divine. Those who share a cup with it must do so in honesty, for it can sense deceit as surely as sharks sense blood.

Sailors once left offerings of rice wine upon the beaches to appease these spirits, hoping for calm seas and safe passage. A flask tipped into the tide was said to ensure fair weather, for the Shōjō favored travelers who honored the ocean's generosity. In some fishing villages, when the waves turned red with algae or sunset reflection, elders murmured that the Shōjō were dancing below — staining the water with their laughter. Even mischief in their presence was considered sacred, for laughter was part of their blessing.

Beneath its revelry lies wisdom. In the Noh tradition, the Shōjō symbolizes sincerity unclouded by pretension. It drinks deeply because it feels deeply; it laughs because it remembers sorrow and chooses joy. In this sense, it stands as the antithesis of the scheming trickster or wrathful demon — a yokai of pure emotion, proof that not all spirits are born from fear. Its wine, endless and golden, represents enlightenment through joy rather than suffering, a truth rare in a world that too often finds wisdom only in pain.

Artists of the Edo period captured its exuberant spirit in bright vermilion pigments and flowing brushstrokes. Woodblock prints show Shōjō frolicking beside waves or raising cups to the moon, while actors in Noh masks dyed crimson dance in slow, graceful spirals — embodying the spirit's laughter as sacred offering. Poets likened the foam of the tide to spilled sake, the sea itself to the great jar from which the Shōjō drinks eternity. Even in stillness, its presence seems to ripple with music.

Over time, the Shōjō became a symbol of honest pleasure and emotional authenticity. In taverns, its name came to mean a lively, ruddy-faced drinker; in art, it remained a reminder that joy can be divine when rooted in truth. Statues of red-haired figures once stood at docks and breweries as talismans for prosperity and harmony.

tengu

animals, guardians and hybrid beasts

feathered spirits of mountain wind

High among the slopes where pine needles shiver and the mists weave between cliffs, the Tengu take flight. With wings like ravens and noses long enough to pierce arrogance, these beings of Japanese lore are as elusive as they are unforgettable. Some appear birdlike, with sharp beaks and feathers ruffling in mountain wind; others have evolved into almost-human warriors with crimson skin and piercing eyes, walking in the robes of mountain priests. The mountain is their home, and they are its will—sometimes guardian, sometimes punisher.

The name Tengu is thought to derive from the Chinese Tiangou, a celestial dog-like spirit, but Japan reimagined the figure entirely. By the Heian period (794–1185), the Tengu were firmly part of native folklore, especially in regions like Mount Kurama and Mount Takao. At first feared as omens of disaster and prideful spirits who lured monks to ruin, their image slowly shifted. Through centuries of religious blending—Shinto, Buddhist, and Shugendō beliefs—Tengu became not just spirits of mischief but also martial protectors and teachers of swordsmanship and ascetic discipline.

The Tengu are usually divided into two classes: Karasu Tengu, who retain more avian features like beaks and wings, and Daitengu, who appear more human with long noses and red skin. Both types dwell in forests and mountains, where they serve as wardens of sacred spaces. Dressed like yamabushi (mountain hermits and warrior monks), they possess deep spiritual power, fly effortlessly, and can wield enchanted fans that summon storms or knock down opponents with a gust. Their appearance in a story often signals a disruption of balance—or a test to be passed.

Stories about the Tengu often involve human arrogance. Proud monks, corrupt officials, or boastful warriors may be tricked, abducted, or chastened by Tengu until they learn humility. One famous tale tells of the warrior Minamoto no Yoshitsune, who is trained in secret martial arts by a Tengu master named Sōjōbō of Mount Kurama. Other tales speak of temples protected from evil by Tengu who take up arms in defense of sacred ground. As with many Japanese yōkai, Tengu exist on a spectrum: they are as much reflection as they are reality.

Over time, the Tengu became complex figures—neither wholly good nor evil. In the Edo period, illustrated woodblock prints and otogi-zōshi tales often depicted them as symbols of contradiction: dangerous if offended, yet wise and noble when honored. Their masks became a staple of Noh theater and festival parades, representing both mystery and martial strength. Their long noses, once symbols of demonic vanity, grew to embody deep spiritual insight—for the Tengu sees far and flies higher than any mortal.

The Tengu's deep connection to mountain asceticism reveals them not as merely physical beings, but as the embodiment of the mountain's discipline. To climb into their realm is to engage in struggle—not against them, but against the illusions one carries. In stories, those who meet Tengu often return changed: physically stronger, spiritually humbled, or psychologically shattered. They are initiators of transformation, hiding their lessons in pranks, riddles, or duels beneath falling pine needles.

umibōzu

animals, guardians and hybrid beasts

sea monk of the storming abyss

When the sea lies quiet and moonlight scatters across the surface, sailors whisper the oldest of fears — that beneath the calm waits the Umibōzu, the Sea Monk. Rising without warning from the depths, it takes the form of a vast, dark figure with a smooth, bald head like a monk's and eyes that glow like lanterns through rain. To glimpse it is to know terror, for its arrival heralds wind, lightning, and waves high enough to swallow ships whole. The sea is its temple, and every storm its sermon.

The legend of the Umibōzu is as ancient as Japan's maritime memory. Its name joins umi (sea) and bōzu (monk), evoking both reverence and dread. Folklore from coastal regions like Tohoku, Kyushu, and the Seto Inland Sea all speak of the same towering specter — some claiming it is the vengeful ghost of a drowned priest, others that it is the sea itself given human form. It appears suddenly on calm nights, rising so tall that even clouds brush its shoulders, and stares silently before destroying the vessel with waves born of its own wrath.

One of the oldest recorded tales, from the Edo period's Hyakkai Zukan and maritime logs, describes sailors seeing a head the size of a mountain rise from the horizon. When they prayed or spoke the name of Buddha, the creature fell still — until one man broke the silence with a curse, and the waves devoured them all. Another account claims that the Umibōzu demanded a bucket from shipmen to scoop water, only for the clever captain to hand it a bucket with a hole in the bottom, saving his crew from drowning. These stories speak of both fear and wit, and the eternal dance between reverence and defiance in the face of the sea's power.

Descriptions of its form vary as wildly as the sea itself. Some Umibōzu appear as featureless black giants whose bodies dissolve into mist above the waves; others have luminous eyes, elongated arms, or robes that flow like ink. The calm voice of a Buddhist monk is said to precede its rise, carried on the wind moments before the storm breaks. Many believe it seeks the prayers of the living, longing for rites denied to those who drowned — souls uncremated, unremembered, returned to the water as vast and restless as the ocean that claimed them.

Spiritually, the Umibōzu stands at the crossroads of reverence and guilt. To sailors, it is a haunting reminder that the sea gives life but demands respect. To priests, it embodies karmic imbalance — the suffering of spirits unbound by ritual. The image of a monk rising from the waves is no accident: it is the reflection of death and devotion entwined, the sacred and the profane returning as one. Some coastal temples still light lanterns for lost fishermen each Obon, believing the glow will keep the Umibōzu appeased.

In art and literature, the Umibōzu looms larger than life — not merely a monster, but a metaphor for the vast unknown. Edo-era scrolls depict it with ink-black contours against crashing surf, its form half-seen, as if even paper could not contain its enormity. Woodblock prints by masters such as Toriyama Sekien capture it as both terrifying and strangely beautiful — a shadow that completes the sea. The Umibōzu became a symbol of nature's sublime power: serene, merciless, divine.

ushioni

animals, guardians and hybrid beasts
ox demon of coastal dread

Along the rocky shores of western Japan, where the tide churns beneath storm clouds and the wind tastes of iron, fishermen once feared the Ushioni — the Ox Demon. It was said to rise from the sea like a shadow of vengeance, half beast and half spirit, its bull's head gleaming with salt and fury. Some claimed it stalked the beaches at dusk, snorting mist and trampling footprints that glowed faintly in the moonlight. Others whispered that it leapt from the waves itself, its cry echoing through the fog like the bellow of a dying god.

The name Ushioni (牛鬼) literally means "ox demon," but the creature's form shifts with each region's memory. In some provinces it bears the full head of an ox upon a spider's body, its many legs scraping the sand; in others, it resembles a bull-headed giant cloaked in kelp, dripping seawater and blood. In every version, it is a creature of pollution and terror — a yokai born from the unholy meeting of land and sea, of human fear and untamed nature. Its eyes are red, its breath foul, its power unmatched among the coastal spirits.

The earliest recorded sightings date back to the Sengoku period, when battles raged across the islands. Soldiers marching near the Seto Inland Sea told of monstrous roars that rose with the tide. They said the Ushioni appeared where too many men had died, feeding upon blood spilled into the ocean. To some, it was the sea's vengeance; to others, a demon drawn to human suffering. The creature's presence heralded plague, shipwreck, and famine — disasters blamed not on gods, but on the wrath of the beast itself.

Yet folklore also holds that the Ushioni was not entirely solitary. In many regions, it traveled with another yokai — the Nure-onna, the serpent woman of the waves. She would lure men to the shore, weeping or calling for help, while the Ushioni waited in the surf. When the victim approached, the sea erupted in black water and teeth. Together, they formed a pair of illusions — beauty and horror intertwined — echoing Japan's belief that the natural world both tempts and devours with equal grace.

Its behavior, though monstrous, reflected a kind of divine logic. The Ushioni despised impurity and intrusion. Travelers who crossed sacred headlands without purification, or fishermen who mocked the sea, were said to draw its fury. Monks who appeased it through prayer described visions of a colossal ox weeping tears of salt, bound to the waves for eternity. In these tales, it became less a predator than a cursed guardian — an embodiment of the boundary between the mortal world and the ocean's abyss.

The people of coastal villages feared and revered it in equal measure. Shrines were raised at cliffs and harbors where the Ushioni was said to dwell. Offerings of sake and white rice were left to calm its spirit, while festivals in Ehime and Kochi celebrated its image in papier-mâché effigies — fierce but smiling, its horns gilded in gold. These rituals transformed terror into protection, turning the demon of the sea into a watchful deity who guarded fishermen from real storms.

Artists and storytellers through the Edo period painted the Ushioni with fascination rather than fear. In scrolls, it stalks moonlit shores under whirling clouds, its many legs treading both air and water. The creature's duality — sacred and unclean, destroyer and protector — captivated poets and monks alike. It became an emblem of the tension between humankind and nature's wild heart, a reflection of how awe and terror intertwine in Japan's coastal mythology.

Printed by Libri Plureos GmbH in Hamburg, Germany